NOT WITHOUT MY NEIGHBOUR

S. WESLEY ARIARAJAH

NOT WITHOUT MY NEIGHBOUR

ISSUES IN INTERFAITH RELATIONS

Risk
BOOK SERIES

WCC PUBLICATIONS, GENEVA

Cover design: Edwin Hassink

ISBN 2-8254-1308-9

© 1999 WCC Publications, World Council of Churches,
150 route de Ferney, 1211 Geneva 2, Switzerland

No. 85 in the Risk Book Series

Printed in Switzerland

To the memory of D.T. Niles and Lynn de Silva –
one taught me the faith,
the other taught me how to relate it

Table of Contents

1. "Not Without
   My Neighbour"

How it all began: the personal journey

When I was a student, our family lived in a seaside town in the north of Sri Lanka called KKS. Now, that is a rather unusual name for a Sri Lankan town! In fact, the actual name is Kankesanthurai, which means the port-town in which the image of Lord Kankesan, a Hindu deity, arrived in Sri Lanka from India. In addition to its rich meaning, there is also a melodious ring to it when one says it in Tamil. But during the colonial days the successive Portuguese, Dutch and British rulers of the island could not correctly pronounce the names of many Sri Lankan towns; for them they were "tongue-twisters". When they could not, or were too lazy to articulate a name, they just changed it or abbreviated it. Thus "Yalpanam", "the town of singers with the harp", became "Jaffna", which meant nothing, and Kankesanthurai, KKS.

What is interesting about KKS was that it was almost entirely a Hindu town. There were a few Roman Catholic families, but we were one of the only two Protestant families. The other family was a single-person "family"; we were six. The church insisted on counting every household as a "family" irrespective of its size. Naturally, no Protestant church was built in KKS. The nearest town that had a church building had no more than three Protestant families in it. We had no pastor of our own, but a "visiting minister". If our family did not turn up for church on a Sunday, and a few others also stayed away, the Sunday service would end up as the pastor's private prayer. Our family made up seventy percent of the congregation, and one hundred percent of the children in it!

We first lived in Jaffna, the capital of northern Sri Lanka, where there was a large, lively and thriving Methodist congregation. We were all born into it. But while I was only five, the family moved because my father's place of work was now at KKS.

The consequence of this is obvious: we were surrounded by Hindu families. As children, we played with the Hindu children, went to school with them, and in keeping with the practice in Asia we were in and out of each other's homes at all times of the day. In fact, our next-door Hindu neighbours' two children regularly joined us in our evening family prayers. The prayers were elaborate affairs in those days, with singing of lyrics and choruses, Bible reading and two or three persons, including children, offering the petitions. The Hindu children loved it, and our neighbours were happy that their children joined us for prayers. Often some of us from the Christian home would be at our neighbours' when they had their *pujas* (the Hindu prayers) and sang the *tevarams* (devotional songs) in the evenings.

My father decided to send me and my older brother to the Methodist boarding school in Jaffna, so that we would have "better education" in a "Christian environment". But we would return to KKS for long weekends and school holidays. Soon, our immediate Hindu neighbours became our closest friends.

As I grew up and began to understand religious matters, I became aware of the differences between Christianity and Hinduism and why we were Christians and not Hindus. But I also became aware that our neighbours were a devout family and that their prayer life was for them profoundly meaningful. Perhaps what impressed me most was that their prayer life appeared to bear fruits. They were an ethically conscious family. They extended warm and loving friendship to us, their neighbours. The fact that we were not Hindus made no difference in their attitude towards us. We were as much their children as their own. And this attitude of openness and friendship extended to others in the neighbourhood as well. Long before I learned theology, and was able to articulate religious matters, I had come to think of them as a family rooted in God's love.

Though I deeply respect Hinduism as a religion and admire several aspects of its insight into life and reality, I was not overly romantic about it then, or even now after studying it at some depth. I knew many Hindu families that were not devout, like many Christian families. Nor does being a Hindu automatically make a person ethically sensitive. In fact, most Hindus in those days thought of Protestant Christians as people of high moral integrity and wanted their children to be associated with us. Moreover, our neighbours were by no means extraordinary people. As a family they too had all the strengths and weaknesses of an average Sri Lankan family. No, we did not have angels for next-door neighbours.

Yet, their religious devotion and the life that came out of it were impressive. We had the opportunity to observe and experience them, not just at close quarters, but almost from the inside. Their family name, Sathasivam, means "the Eternal One is ever present with us". It was a fitting name.

The one and the many

When I became a young adult and had more serious involvement in the Christian faith in the student movement, church study groups and the like, I began to hear more and more about "mission". The general position, often repeated, went along these lines: All human beings are sinners and are alienated from God. We can never hope to achieve our salvation through our own efforts. But God, out of God's goodness and grace, has revealed God's nature to us in the life of Jesus. And Jesus, through his death and resurrection, has opened the way of salvation. As Christians, we already have this salvation offered to us as a free gift. Now it is our responsibility to preach the gospel and pass on this good news to our Hindu neighbours and bring them also to Christ.

"What about the Hindus who pray and have a loving relationship with their neighbours and lead an ethically upright life?", I would ask in the study group.

"Of course there are good Hindus, and we must respect them," came the answer, rather grudgingly. "But as religious persons, they are misguided; they do not know the true God. In any case, unless they confess Christ and believe in him they cannot be saved."

The hard-nosed gospel-preachers, who often held open-air meetings in the Jaffna stadium in those days, went even further and would describe the Hindus as "idol worshippers" and "superstitious". While we Christians are assured of heaven, they would say, the Hindus, who do not believe, will certainly go to hell. Therefore, there is an urgency about the need to share the gospel with the Hindus and call them to follow Christ.

That is what the Bible, the word of God, teaches us, the preacher would say, quoting chapters and verses from memory.

Who can argue with the Bible?

But I was torn apart by such a message.

I was, by then, a convinced Christian and was part of Bible study groups, prayer cells and the like. I was among the students at the boarding school whom the missionary, stationed in Jaffna, would send to the town and the nearby villages to distribute scripture portions and evangelistic pamphlets. I also became aware that, more often than not, the Hindus did not readily "respond" and become Christians. They would respectfully listen to us and converse with us, but rarely went further.

Will my Hindu neighbours at KKS indeed go to hell because they are not Christians? Are they in fact not in a relationship with God? What do we make of their devotional life and all that has come out of it?

At that time I could not make any theological sense of the problem; nor did I have the tools to do so. But I "felt", somewhere deep down, that it would be unfair on the part of God to receive us, the Christian family, into heaven and send our next-door Hindu neighbours to hell. It was inconceivable to me; it was clearly unfair. I wouldn't want to be in a heaven where our neighbours were not.

Only recently I read the book, also made into a film, *Not Without My Daughter*, dealing of course with a very different subject. I have had some difficulty with both, for I feared that they would reinforce some of the caricatures of Islam prevalent today. But I found in the title of the book and the film an apt echo of the strong feelings that I had, some forty years earlier, when I heard some of the preachers speak of salvation and of heaven and hell. It was then a "feeling" which could neither be articulated nor theologically resolved.

The present title, "Not Without My Neighbour", inspired by the title of the other book, represents not only my struggle, but the dilemma of many Christians in Asia who live among neighbours of other faiths, and sense in the life of those neighbours something of what is conveyed by the phrase "life in God". Often their relationships are so close and their perception of the spiritual life of the "other" is such that they do not want to be in a "heaven" to which their neighbours are denied admission. It is for them, as it is for me, a moral dilemma.

Today we no longer speak the language of our "going to heaven" and their "going to hell." We know about myths and symbols employed in religious language to indicate deeper realities. Most of us have also outgrown the need to speak of these realities in spatial metaphors like "heaven" and "hell". We have learned to respect other people's faiths and would rarely, if ever, call the Hindus "idol worshippers". In some parts of the church, theology and the theology of religions have also been "expanded" to accommodate the reality of persistent plurality and the resurgence of other religions. Interfaith dialogue and interfaith cooperation have come into vogue.

But deep down, have we really resolved the spiritual and theological tension I experienced as a young adult? Has the church made up its mind on my Hindu neighbours' religious life?

I doubt it.

To continue my story, my own interests went in two directions. On the one hand, under the influence of great Christian teachers and preachers, including the great ecumenist D.T. Niles, who was my pastor at the Jaffna church for six years and prepared me and my friends for confirmation, my Christian faith became even stronger and I went into the Methodist ministry. On the other hand, I decided, perhaps unconsciously, not to let the spiritual dilemma about my Hindu neighbours go unexplored. Therefore, I also undertook an in-depth study of Hinduism and Buddhism, the two prominent religions of Sri Lanka, to which 85 percent of the people belonged. I became interested in interfaith dialogue, led in Sri Lanka by another ecumenical veteran, Lynn de Silva.

All these finally led me to the dialogue programme of the World Council of Churches, and eventually to take over the staff position in the Dialogue sub-unit left vacant by the retirement of Stanley Samartha. Dr Samartha, who had pioneered the dialogue ministry of the WCC and had given it his leadership during the formative and difficult days, had been my own teacher in Hinduism and Indian philosophy. The transition from the guru to the student went rather smoothly.

Why yet another book?

WCC's publications editor, and also my colleague and friend, Marlin VanElderen, asked me when I left the staff of the WCC after sixteen years to consider writing a book to "gather up" my work on dialogue at the WCC. This was a kind and generous invitation, and I readily accepted.

But did we need another book on interfaith dialogue or religious pluralism? There are many good books today on this subject, and the whole attitude of dialogical relationships with neighbours of other faith traditions is widely accepted in much of the church constituency. I felt there was no need for yet another book to convince people of the importance of dialogue or explain how it might be pursued.

But the whole relationship of dialogue, especially during the last decade, has thrown up several issues that are in need of further exploration. What have the WCC's own work and contributions been on these issues, and how may they be pursued in the churches in the years ahead? Such a discussion, I thought, would be of some value.

Hence the sub-title, "Issues in Interfaith Dialogue".

I had to make a selection of issues for the present discussion. Another person, from another background, might have selected a different set of issues as demanding greater attention today. There is no intention on my part to be definitive or exhaustive. My only hope is that the discussion here will animate the ongoing debate of these concerns in the churches, or help begin it where it is not already in place. We, as Christians, indeed people of any faith tradition for that matter, can no longer afford to be ill-equipped to face the interfaith reality.

Those who are familiar with the dialogue concern will be aware that over the past two decades hundreds of books have appeared in the fields of dialogue, religious plurality, Christology, theology of religions and related issues, seeking to explore these concerns in various ways. It is part of my job to read as many of these books as I possibly can, and the temptation to discuss them is almost irresistible. The literature is as rich as it is diverse. But I have opted here to stay with the discussions within the WCC and its ecumenical partners, partly to limit our immediate interest to conversations and events in which I was myself directly involved during my time with the WCC.

In the sermon he preached at his consecration as Archbishop of Canterbury in 1942, William Temple spoke of the decision of the churches to work for unity as "the great new fact" of our era. He was a man of great discernment. Had he lived today, I am convinced that he would have spoken of the forces that draw religions together as the "great new fact" of our day, which we dare not ignore.

Five phases of the dialogue work

Looking back at the brief history of the dialogue work within the WCC, one may identify five phases, layers or dimensions that are inter-related. Each one of them has had some prominence at different periods of history, but they also happen concurrently and feed on one another.

The initial phase of work centred on the concept of dialogue itself. After a long history of discussions on the nature of our relationships with neighbours of other religious traditions, "dialogue" emerged as an appropriate concept to describe that relationship. But the very concept challenged some of the entrenched theological perceptions of the church, leading to prolonged debates and considerable literature on what dialogue is and what it is not, what it affirmed, and what it did not deny. On the whole, the search for "community" with neighbours of other faiths is the goal which that debate set for dialogue, although not everyone agreed on the meaning of the word "community", or what it entailed.

This debate, however, opened up several questions about our own faith and its formulations. What does "mission" mean within this new relationship? How do Christians understand religious plurality? How do we understand the significance of Christ and what we believe God has done in Christ within this relationship? Thus the second phase is one that pushed us back to our own faith to find adequate foundations for the new relationship and to restate our faith for that relationship.

The new approach also meant new institutional relations. The dialogue programme of the WCC opened up new contacts with the world Jewish, Islamic, Buddhist organizations and with corresponding partners in other religions. Also of significance are the contacts with international interfaith organizations such as the World Conference on Religion and Peace (WCRP), the World Congress of Faiths and the International Association for Religious Freedom (IARF), and participation in significant world interfaith events, as for example the second Parliament of World's Religions in Chicago, and the commemoration of the first Parliament in several places, especially in Bangalore. These were accompanied by actual dialogue meetings at the international level, organized by the sub-unit, and the promotion of dialogue at local levels.

The attempts to promote dialogue at local levels brought up several pastoral issues that needed attention. "Is it all right to engage in interfaith worship? How do we go about it?" "How do we handle marriages across religious traditions? Are they to be encouraged as occasions for the dialogue of life?" "How do we deal with militant expressions of religion and the suppression of religious minorities? At what point do we stop the dialogue and confront our neighbours?" "Should we dialogue with neighbours who do not respect the rights of women as we understand them?" "How do we engage in a dialogue on justice and issues of human rights?" These are tough, but relevant, immediate and down-to-earth issues that need attention. They constitute the fourth dimension of the dialogue work.

In more recent years we also entered in our dialogue with our neighbours on what might be tentatively called "the future of religion and religions". We live in a world where changes take place at an unprecedented pace. The globalization of many aspects of life and revolutions in technology and communications would no doubt leave their mark also on religious belief and practice. What would be the impact of the rising secular, technological and global "culture" on all our religions and religious life? These issues are pertinent to all religions as well as to their relationships with one another. This fifth phase of a joint exploration has begun, but it is only in its initial stages.

There are several issues in each of these five areas that are worth exploring and stand in need of exploration. I have, however, concentrated primarily on the pastoral area. In each case, in addition to introducing the issue, I have also dealt with my own thoughts on it. They will of course be challenged by others, and thus open up a dialogue on the issue. My intention is not to provide answers. Who can indeed provide answers to such complex questions? On each issue, however, I have followed a particular line of conviction so that it might provide a basis for dialogue. It is important to note that the positions I take are not the positions of the WCC or its dialogue programme, but considerations that come out of my own experience in the dialogue field.

In the last chapter, "Dialogue or Mission", I have followed a different approach and quote more extensively from conference documents and reports. This is done on purpose to provide more documentation on the issue which continues to engage the church, even as "evangelistic fervour" rises in many places as a response to the approach of a new millennium.

What, then, are some of the issues that face the interfaith movement as it seeks to draw people together into a new relationship? And what has been the contribution of the WCC's dialogue programme to them?

We begin with a question that troubles many people today: the rise of fundamentalism and militant expressions of religion.

2. Dialogue and Conflict: Are There Limits to Dialogue?

I remember the day I received a fax marked "urgent" from Subramaniya Swami, the editor of *Hinduism Today*, a periodical that seeks to serve the interests of Hindus who now live in significant numbers in many parts of the world. The periodical attempts to do many things: to serve as a link among the Hindus scattered around the world, to deal with the basic teachings of Hinduism, to give news and information on Hindus and Hinduism, and to highlight and advocate Hindu concerns. Swamiji's faxed message now had to do with this last aspect of the functions of the periodical.

The subject was the situation in Fiji, the Pacific island with which the WCC has had close relationships since its inception. Fiji's problem, like that of so many other countries in different parts of the world, has to do with its colonial past. During the colonial days the British had brought a large number of labourers from India to work in the sugar plantations. Over the years, through sheer numerical increase, people of Indian origin comprised almost half the population of the island.

Native Fijians owned the land. Indians had gradually grown into a community that exercised considerable influence in finance, trade and industry. Most native Fijians were Christians. Most of the Fijians of Indian origin were Hindus and Muslims. Their economic influence now meant political power as well, which led to conflicts in the island and heightened ethnic tensions.

The scenario is not new. We have it in the Bible when "a new king arose in Egypt who did not know Joseph". He said to the people, "Look, the Israelite people are more numerous and more powerful than we." He decided to deal with them harshly to check the rising "threat" (Ex. 1:8ff.).

The immediate context of the fax was a situation of tension precipitated by a group of young people who, after an all-night prayer vigil(!), had descended in the early hours of the morning on a Hindu temple and an Islamic mosque and set them on fire. What had the WCC to say on this, and what action did it propose to take?

This is only one example of the instances of religion-related intolerance, tension, open conflict and even killings that are brought to the attention of the WCC, often with the question, "What does the dialogue programme of the WCC plan to do about this?" Provocation came from both sides. At times Christians had acted violently, as in the case of Fiji, or had disrupted the life of other communities by preventing the building of a place of worship in a traditionally Christian area, or refused to allow the teaching of other religions in a school, or supported and encouraged the enactment of laws in the parliament that discriminated against minority religions.

There were instances where Christians raised complaints about other religious groups: of burning down of churches in Nigeria, of being denied the right to practise their religion, or of false accusations brought against them under blasphemy laws.

In each case, one first had to try to establish the facts, and get in touch with the church and religious leaders as well as our dialogue partners in the concerned country to make an assessment of the situation and to recommend an appropriate response by the WCC. Sometimes fact-finding or pastoral visits are organized. In the case of Fiji, in addition to making clear statements and initiating the necessary contacts with the churches and leaders of other religious communities, the WCC sent a multifaith team to visit all the religious communities and to strengthen the hand of the Interfaith Search, a local dialogue group that was seeking to promote dialogue and understanding among all the communities involved.[1]

When people at the end of a lecture or in a seminar came out with the question "What is the dialogue programme doing about..." this or that conflict situation, I always had a "stock answer" to give, borrowed from the medical field: "Dialogue is not an ambulance service; it is a public health programme!" Though not fully satisfied with what appears to be an evasive response, people eventually get the point. The truth of the statement had come home to me powerfully when I was pastoring a Methodist congregation in Colombo, the capital of Sri Lanka.

One of Sri Lanka's periodic ethnic conflicts broke out in 1978 soon after a parliamentary election. Enormous suffering was inflicted on one ethnic group by sections of the other. Many hundreds, including some from my own congregation, had to flee for their lives and seek shelter in makeshift "refugee camps" – schools, temples and churches.

As the violence was subsiding, I received a telephone call asking me to attend a meeting of the religious leaders of the area to explore how we might attempt to promote peace within the community. Buddhist, Hindu, Muslim and Christian (Roman Catholic and Protestant) clergy of the area and some prominent lay persons from each of the religious communities had been brought together "to take urgent action" to "promote peace and harmony" in the community.

Though well-meant, it struck me as a pointless exercise. In the first place, it turned out that most of the clergy of the area were meeting one another for the very first time. Despite the series of ethnic conflicts in the country since 1958, so far hardly any group had made an effort to promote harmony among the people. I was certain that none of the religious groups present had tried to teach their religion "in relation to" the other, only as "superior" to others', calling for the total allegiance of its adherents. I felt that there was a yawning gap between how we had conducted ourselves during peace time and what we were now setting out to do. The effort, though it had to be undertaken, lacked credibility. We were doing ambulance service where public health education and immunization were called for long before the outbreak of the disease!

Attempting to promote dialogue or intercommunal, interfaith harmony during or soon after a conflict, though it has its own limited value, is a frustrating exercise. Communities by now are deeply polarized, confused and uncertain about who can be trusted. Solidarity across to the other community is often misunderstood as betrayal.

Efforts to bring about peace and reconciliation do have their legitimate place in such situations, but they call for different methods and skills.

Dialogue is not so much about attempting to resolve immediate conflicts, but about building a "community of

14

conversation", a "community of heart and mind" across racial, ethnic and religious barriers where people learn to see differences among them not as threatening but as "natural" and "normal". Dialogue thus is an attempt to help people to understand and accept the other in their "otherness". It seeks to make people "at home" with plurality, to develop an appreciation of diversity, and to make those links that may just help them to hold together when the whole community is threatened by forces of separation and anarchy.

Intolerance and fundamentalism

But the concerns of this chapter run deeper. What of the rise of fundamentalism in almost all religions, of the increasing use of religion in politics, of planned attacks on a religious community to intimidate it and to dominate it? At what point do we call off the dialogue? Isn't it naive to advocate dialogue in situations where what is called for is actual confrontation, challenge and, where necessary, concerted action to protect a community?

This appeared to be the situation in Nigeria some years ago. Writing in *Current Dialogue*, the publication of the dialogue programme of the WCC, Josiah Idowu-Fearon, an Anglican bishop in the Muslim-dominated northern Nigeria, gives the following table of events between 1991 and 1992:

> April 1991: Bauchi, an ethnic misunderstanding degenerated into a full-blown religious war between Muslims and Christians; thousands died.
> October 1991: Religious riots in Kano to protest the crusade of Reinhard Bonnke; some thousand people died.
> March 1992: Muslim and Christian students riot in Jalingo; over one hundred died.
> May 1992: Another ethnic misunderstanding in Zangon-Kataf degenerated into a religious battle between Muslims and Christians which spread into Kaduna and Zaria. Over 3000 died.[2]

The fuller account actually lists intercommunal conflicts since the 1980s, including such provocative acts as in May 1986 when a group of religious fanatics set fire to a wooden sculpture of Jesus Christ in the university chapel. The victims were not only Christians but also many Muslims who became the objects of reprisal killings.

There was no dearth of attempts on the part of the government and religious groups to do something about it. In 1987 the federal government set up an advisory council on religious affairs. In the same year a group of intellectuals, drawn from the different groups, came together to form what was known as the National Association for Religious and Ethnic Tolerance. In 1992 the federal government set up yet another body called the Centre for Religious and Ethnic Tolerance.[3]

But tension, mutual suspicion and their periodic outbursts into open conflict continued.

Nigeria is by no means the only country where there has been increasing religious tension especially between Christians and Muslims. Sudan, Bosnia, Pakistan and Malaysia are among the other states that have drawn the attention of the WCC. There were also continuing conflicts as in the Middle East, Northern Ireland, former Yugoslavia, Sri Lanka, India and other places, where other religious traditions were involved and where religious sentiments played a significant role in giving identity to communities in conflict.

I have chosen Nigeria as an example to illustrate the complexity of some of these conflicts which are too easily identified as "religious conflicts" by many, including the mass media.

Bishop Josiah points out that the Nigerian problem is also a part of its colonial legacy. Nigeria as a "nation" existed only in the imagination of the British colonizers and for their convenience. Some claim this to be the situation even today. A columnist in the *Nigerian Tribune* writes: "Nigeria is not a nation; it is a conglomeration of tribal groups. It is an artificial set-up, kept together by the persuasion of our overseas creditors and the major powers who use it as a large marketplace for dumping their manufactured goods. The Nigerian himself has no sense of belonging, no national consciousness. His loyalty is to his tribe... It is the truth which we must acknowledge."[4]

The artificial bringing together of distinct tribal groups through outside pressure was further complicated by the bringing together of the Northern and Southern regions. The North, 90 percent Muslim, lived under the shari'a even during the British period, while the South was 80 percent Christian. The "Nigeria" thus created, in the opinion of many, was a "geographical expression" rather than a nation-state. "I believe", wrote another columnist in the *Nigerian Tribune*, "the Nigerian problem is that of state creation; state here referring to the nation state, in which strange bedfellows were brought together by the British colonial masters with no regard whatsoever for political and ethnic affinity... What we call Nigeria today is actually two countries married together not only against their will, but to their mutual disadvantage."[5]

My intention is not to further criticize the colonial record. Much has been said on that subject. Nor can all the ills of a nation be traced back to its colonial heritage. But the historical background is important in each specific situation. It reveals the complex factors involved in intercommunity relations and shows the differences among them. In the dialogue field we cannot ignore the fact that religious traditions, in addition to providing a spiritual basis for life, are also sociological realities, and that they have been used, misused and abused throughout history by power groups in the social and political fields to achieve ends that have little to do with human well-being. Nor can we forget that religions themselves have been the bastions of ideological persuasions, and power groups within religion have grossly misled people of their own fold and beyond.

Merely to state that "Muslims are killing Christians" in Nigeria or "Christians are killing Muslims in Bosnia" involves an over-simplification. Although religious affiliation or background provides a collective identity to the group, most conflicts are caused by a combination of historical, ethnic, tribal, racial, economic and political factors that call for closer analysis and considered response.

This does not mean, of course, that religious traditions have no role in conflict situations. There are several instances where a majority religious community is seen as supporting the suppression of a minority religious group. There are differing and conflicting understandings among religions on the relationship between religion and state, and on religion and law. Some of the serious misunderstandings, especially between Western Christians and Muslims, stem from different perceptions of the role of religion in politics and in the affairs of the state. Islam does not see religion as belonging to the "private sphere" but as providing the basis on which the totality of life – religious, social and political – should be organized. Therefore, on the basis of the historical experiences that shaped the origin and development of Islam, living under the shari'a, when it is rightly administered, is not an imposition of hardship but a call to organize society on firm religious and moral foundations. To the Western cultures which, based on a different historical experience, have separated the political, judicial and religious spheres, the bringing together of these constitutes a threat.

In a similar manner, Muslims and Christians have also disagreed on the issue of human rights, particularly on the relationship between the rights of the individual and those of the community. These differences have led to mutual accusations, Western Christians accusing Islam of not doing justice to individual freedoms and human rights, and Islam accusing the Christian West of building society on a secular basis, divorced from religious principles, thus leading to excessive individualism, materialism and the erosion of life in community.

All this is not meant to apportion blame for the deteriorating relationships or to commend any particular strategy that is likely to bring about social cohesion and peace within and between communities. What is most important today is the knowledge, acknowledgment and acceptance that there are different foundations on which societies are organized, and that none of them has been able to produce the ideal society. Such a society may indeed exist in the scriptures, philosophies or ideologies that provide the inspiration, but a cursory look at all our histories will reveal the failures, gaps and misadventures. Perhaps we have much to learn from one another's experiences.

It is significant that the WCC's Christian-Muslim dialogue programme, under the leadership of Tarek Mitri, undertook in recent years the difficult task of bringing together protagonists of the different positions on such matters for a series of meetings. Thus meetings were held on the question of shari'a with Islamic lawyers (also from countries governed according to the shari'a) and Christian lawyers who advocate a different form of social governance. This gave the opportunity to both sides to go beyond "shadow boxing" and mutual recrimination in absentia to real engagement on the promises and limits of any system that seeks to shape the life of a community for its total well-being.

Similarly Christians and Muslims met on the issue of minorities to examine the provisions made in their respective religious traditions and how they are being implemented or sidelined, especially with a plan to set up a mechanism by which we can call one another to account. A Muslim-Christian meeting was also organized to tackle the difficult issue of human rights, including the rights and responsibilities of women and men in society. In yet another event, Christians and Muslims from countries where there is discernible tension or open conflict between the two communities were brought together to explore the underlying reasons for confrontation and what realistic options were open to those committed to justice and peace within both communities.

All these were fruitful ventures. When an atmosphere of trust is created there will be willingness to be open, to consider the positions of the other, to engage in self-criticism and constructive criticism of the other, to look for ways to learn from one another, and to recognize the importance of living creatively with our differences.

A city of peace or dissension?

A similar significant initiative was undertaken by Hans Ucko, who is responsible for WCC's Christian-Jewish relations. With the "advancement" of the Middle-East peace process (inch by inch) the difficult problem of Jerusalem must receive close and patient attention. The city has enormous religious significance for Jews, Christians and Muslims. It is impossible for any political development truly to succeed if it does not reckon with the city's historical importance to the three religious traditions related to it. Will Jerusalem always remain a divided city of conflict and chaos? Will it ever be the "city of peace" as envisioned in all three religions associated with it? One contribution that could be made, especially in view of the conflicting historical perceptions, mutual accusations and recriminations which have marked much of the way in which claims are made for the city, was to give opportunities to the religious communities involved to listen to one another on "the spiritual significance of Jerusalem" for each of their religious traditions. Two such meetings were organized in collaboration with the Pontifical Council for Inter-religious Dialogue, the Holy See's Commission for Religious Relations with the Jews, and the Lutheran World Federation.

The question of Jerusalem is complex particularly because of the multiple readings of the history of the Middle East. If one feels sceptical of the statement that "there is no neutral reading of history", one should read the history of the Middle East as internalized by the different groups of people who have lived and continue to live there. Moreover, Jerusalem's political significance increasingly overshadows the spiritual one. There was, naturally, wide divergence of views at the meeting on how to deal with the multiplicity of claims about its spiritual significance. What impresses me most in such situations where we bring together people who are supposedly deeply divided is the capacity that gradually emerges within the group which makes it possible for them to speak together with collective pronouns like "we", "our" and "us", as in the preamble to their joint statement:

> ...Through the sharing of the collective memories of our respective traditions, we have gained a deep insight into the uniqueness of Jerusalem and its meaning for us. We have affirmed that

this holy city holds universal spiritual significance to all for whom the ultimate truth is the God of Abraham.

Our passionate debates have also made it clear that there are strongly held views which still threaten to divide us. Likewise acts of violence threaten to tear apart the rich fabric of faith and life in this holy city.

In the face of suspicion and fear which have created a sense of hopelessness among our peoples, we are determined to raise up signs of hope that the city of Jerusalem might yet be a city of peace and reconciliation.

In this we turn to the one just and merciful God who is worshipped by Jews, Christians and Muslims alike. It is this one God who has shared with us the gift of Jerusalem so that we might share it with one another...

The joint statement, about parts of which some participants expressed reservations, and which had to be sensitive to the political realities on the ground, though notable in many respects, was not the main achievement of the meeting. What is significant on all such occasions is the fact of the meeting itself: the listening, the learning and the consequent development of the "we" language. However, it also provided the opportunity to put into words (as the first point of the joint statement does) positions vaguely held but confirmed now by being expressed:

We affirm the holiness of the city of Jerusalem for all three faiths and recognize the rights of all to worship in their own ways. We affirm that the claims that we make in the names of our traditions must not be mutually exclusive.[6]

I have dealt with these concrete examples (Sri Lanka, Nigeria and Jerusalem) primarily to get to the difficult question posed for this chapter: Are there limits to dialogue? When does one call off the dialogue and seek to confront the partner?

One of the difficulties in dealing with the question is the either/or assumption that clouds so much of our thinking. Dialogue does not mean that a community or an individual refrains from going to the court of law to seek justice when a specific right is violated by others. It does not mean that one does not protest against and call to account those who perpetrate violence against a community. Dialogue is not a call to suffer in silence for the sake of peace and harmony. As the prophet Jeremiah says, treating "the wounds of the people carelessly, saying 'peace, peace' when there is no peace" can only bring greater calamities (Jer. 8:11).

Dialogue, therefore, is an attempt not to gloss over but to go deeper into the issues that divide people, causing disharmony and conflict. It is based on the belief that confrontation and conflict will not resolve but only further alienate people from each other. It builds on the experience that many of the conflicts feed on ignorance and prejudice, and that an informed understanding of one's neighbour's perspective and experience is an important component of living in community. Dialogue can also help us to identify and expose the social, economic and political forces that manipulate and abuse our religious sentiments in order to keep us apart or even in conflict for the advancement of selfish ends. Even a "failed" dialogue, where a people end up in deep disagreement and at times break up with no acceptable positions to report on, can go a long way in changing perceptions, attitudes and lives.

In other words, if we are indeed committed to justice and peace, and are convinced of the need to struggle towards a reconciled human community, we seem to have no real alternative to dialogue. Some time back a book appeared with the provocative title *Dialogue or Death*. One may not perhaps want to put it so starkly, but it does point to an important truth. Where dialogue ends, the forces of darkness take over. And it applies to the religious as much as to the social and political spheres.

We must, however, persist with the question, What about fundamentalism and the militant expression of religion? What has dialogue to say about this?

Again, much has been written recently on this issue and all that one can hope to do here is to point to some of the considerations that have influenced the way the WCC has approached the issue. For the sake of brevity I will list these considerations without going into detail:

a) In dealing with these concerns, it is important to recognize not only the plurality of religions but also the plurality *within* religions. It is sometimes surprising to listen to persons who are well aware of the plurality of Christianity – Orthodoxy, Roman Catholicism, and numerous expressions of Protestantism and Pentecostalism, with their own forms of church governance and different positions on crucial doctrinal and ethical issues – speak of Islam or Hinduism as if they were monolithic entities. Hinduism has within it religious expressions that range from atheism to strict monism, monotheism and polytheism. Islam, although it believes in the *umma* (the Islamic community) that cuts across geographical boundaries (as the church does), has great internal diversity in the interpretation and application of the faith that flows out of its primary sources. Islam, like Christianity, is also culturally diverse. Islam in Morocco, Iran, India, Indonesia and China, although part of the one faith, is not the same.

This is an important consideration. When someone has problems with Christianity, Islam or Hinduism, it is important to sort out what we are talking about. Consciousness of this can bring greater clarity amidst the confusions that prevail. The mass media's practice of labelling people and dumping them into categories has gone a long way in shaping perceptions that now need to be fought and overcome.

b) Fundamentalism is not peculiar to any one religious tradition, although it becomes pronounced in various societies at different moments in history. Sri Lankans who are concerned over the rise of Hindu nationalism in India are often not conscious of the impact of Buddhist nationalism on the political life of Sri Lanka and the way it fuels the ethnic conflict. Many people in the United States who are opposed to the rise of Islamic fundamentalism are unaware of, or choose to ignore, the prominent role that the "religious right" plays in US politics. The word "fundamentalism" in fact has a Protestant origin; it denoted a movement within Protestant

Christianity to return to the fundamentals of faith. Its predominantly negative connotation is of more recent origin. Religious fundamentalism, also as a sociological phenomenon, has always existed in history. Expressions of fundamentalism need to be observed, studied and responded to as both religious and political phenomena, in much the same way as we respond to other movements in society. But it is important to recognize that in all religions fundamentalism is no more than one stream among many others.

c) The role of religion in society and its political life is a complex one; it is based on different understandings of religion itself. All religions, at different periods of history, have functioned as catalysts of social transformation, even of social and political revolutions. In contemporary history several positive social and political transformations have been brought about in which religion, religious sentiment or appeal to religion as the rallying force of identity have played a significant role. Thus the role of religion in politics has not always been negative, and one should also be aware that there are situations where religion becomes guilty of complicity by remaining silent or neutral in oppressive situations.

But religion can also be used and abused, as it is in some societies overtly and in others more subtly, in the struggle for political power, in the control and manipulation of the masses, and in maintaining unjust systems. It is important to be aware of the various factors at work when any given conflict is labelled as "religious" conflict. Religion cannot be practised in a vacuum; it cannot be isolated from or independent of socio-political and cultural realities.

Much more can and needs to be said if one were to seek to satisfy those who ask the questions with which I began this chapter, mainly because of the diversity of experiences, the particular circumstances and the actual life-and-death issues which people face in real life. A generalized treatment of the subject of social conflicts does not do justice to many actual situations. The specific response appropriate to any given situation cannot be predetermined or prescribed. Each community must make its own response in its given situation, bearing in mind that it is as important to build up and rally the forces of good as it is to resist evil.

A scene from the film version of *Murder in the Cathedral* has a line that has stayed with me: "The kingdom of God, like any other kingdom, must be defended." So saying, Archbishop Thomas Becket goes into the cathedral to say the mass and to meet what awaits him.

Dialogue, without turning a blind eye to evil, seeks to build on the good; it is an activity related to the building up of the reign of God.

The challenge of dialogue

Much of the criticism of dialogue in this context arises also out of a romanticized understanding of "dialogue". Some think that "everything can be solved if only the parties concerned would sit down and have a dialogue". If the examples given above are anything to go by, it is clear that serious dialogue also calls for serious study, analysis, discernment and the capacity to cut through the superficial and the "fronts" that beguile, to arrive at the heart of the matters that divide us, and seek to face them with honesty. True dialogue is a challenging encounter; it is not for the fainthearted.

Dr Samartha says that building community, like building a good city, takes time, effort and planning. One needs to lay pipelines to bring in fresh water as well as gutters to drain off the waste. A city needs places to do serious work as well as parks and playgrounds and meeting places.

At a seminar in Colombo a participant described how relationships between the communities in conflict had soured over the years. He felt there was no hope of arriving at a settlement in the foreseeable future. He said that in such a situation any advocacy for dialogue appeared to be both naive and misplaced. "Do we still need to advocate dialogue in spite of the fact that our communities are so much alienated from each other?", he asked. He was reacting to a presentation that advocated dialogue.

The speaker who made the presentation responded without a moment's hesitation: "Yes, indeed yes," he said, "not only in spite of it, but also because of it."

NOTES

[1] See Hans Ucko, "Report of an Inter-religious Team Visit to Fiji, 2-10 June 1994", *Current Dialogue*, no. 27, Dec. 1994.
[2] Josiah Idowu-Fearon, "Religious Conflicts in Nigeria", *Current Dialogue*, no. 23, Dec. 1992, p.11.
[3] *Ibid.*, pp.11-12.
[4] *Nigerian Tribune*, 19 Aug. 1992, p.15.
[5] 25 Aug. 1992, p.19. Both quotations are from Bishop Josiah's article cited above.
[6] For the full text of the final communiqué see: "The Spiritual Significance of Jerusalem: a Final Communiqué", in *Current Dialogue*, no. 24, June 1993, pp.10-12.

3. Dialogue and Spirituality: Can We Pray Together?

When I was minister of the Moor Road Methodist church in the southern part of Colombo, I had in my congregation a person by the name of Retnanantham, who had retired as a railway engineer and now spent most of his time promoting interfaith understanding, especially between Christians and Hindus. During my early years in Colombo, he introduced me to a number of Hindu groups. They would invite me during the Christmas and Easter seasons to bring the message of these Christian festivals to hundreds of Hindus who gathered for their weekly worship events. When I asked my friend if the Hindus would not feel "nervous" about asking a Christian minister to speak at their worship events on the basic tenets of the Christian faith, he would simply say: "No, it is no problem because they know that you are a 'dialogue person'!"

I recall those events now, some two decades later, with a measure of surprise. My talk would come in the middle of the *bhajan*, the singing together of devotional songs. On such occasions I would begin with a story from Hindu mythology or with some scriptural references or sayings from Hinduism to create the ambience, and not to be too discontinuous with what was going on. I would, however, talk about the significance of Christmas and Easter for Christians, also indicating the universal significance we attach to these events. Even though I always "preached the gospel" (for what else can one do on the themes of Christmas and Easter?), they continued to invite me, also to speak on other occasions – a courtesy they do not normally extend to Christian ministers.

I wish now, twenty years later, that I had asked for their definition of a "dialogue person". I wonder what Retnanantham had told them a Methodist minister who is also a "dialogue person" would do and not do in a Hindu worship context. I left Colombo in 1978, without ever asking that question. Retnanantham died a few years ago.

But I have always admired the courage and strength of the Hindu worshipping community in its openness to receiving the Christian message. Hinduism is indeed a tolerant and hospitable religion, but here more than hospitality was at work.

As mentioned earlier, at the personal level I had been introduced to hospitality at one another's worship already at KKS, when the next-door children would join us at family prayers, and we from the Christian family were always welcome to be present at the evening Hindu *puja*. But as a minister, I could not return such hospitality to Hindu groups in Colombo and ask their leader to come and give the message of *Deepavali*, *Sivarathiri* or *Krishna Jeyanthi* and other significant Hindu festivals at a Christian worship service or even at a monthly prayer meeting in a Christian home.

I might ask the Hindu Swami from the Ramakrishna mission or the Buddhist monk from the Wellawatte Vihara to speak in the church hall on "national reconciliation" or "world peace". But if I were to ask them to speak on the teachings of Sri Ramakrishna or the Lord Buddha, it would provoke strong protests in the congregation. I was aware that some members of the congregation were not too happy that "their minister" was "present at Hindu worship", even if it was to give the Easter message. They would rather it was done in the market square.

In such a context a Christian worshipping or even praying with a Hindu, Buddhist or Muslim would be considered by many Christians as a "betrayal" of faith or, if they are in a more charitable mood, as a "dilution" of faith.

Why such hesitation?

Why are most Christians hesitant about participating in the worship or an act of prayer that originates from another faith tradition?

Five areas can be lifted up as reasons at the root of much of the objection. I would characterize these as theological, biblical, liturgical, cultural and psychological.

The *theological* reasons for the especially Protestant Christian reluctance to engage in worship with a person of another faith stem from a negative evaluation of other religious traditions as human attempts to find God. They are not based on God's self-revelation, and are therefore expressions of human sin and self-centredness. When approached from this theological perspective, the prayer life of these religions, according to some Christians, is "not valid", "not directed to the true God", "superstitious"; and their prayers are "not appropriate for us, because they are not directed through Jesus Christ".

Such a blanket negative evaluation of other faiths creates many problems for our understanding of God, the nature of God and God's providence, and for our belief in the Holy Spirit as the "giver of life". Such an evaluation of other faiths directly questions one of the streams within the Bible that unambiguously affirms the universal communion between God and all of God's creation.

The negative attitude, however, is deep-rooted, and I have noticed that Christians develop ad hoc theological asides to deal with the issue. Some Christians, though deeply committed to monotheism, live with a "functional polytheism", assuming that the Hindu and the Muslim are praying to "other gods". Others insist that while their prayers may be sincere, a "proper understanding of God" is necessary in order for the prayer to be effective, which of course they do not find in other traditions. At the extreme end there are those who even today would claim that prayers not directed through Christ are "misguided" and are "of the devil". To pray with others is, for them, the ultimate theological compromise that destroys all the rationale for the Christian faith, its witness and mission. In relation to Buddhism, where one cannot discern a clear doctrine of God, common prayer would amount to apostasy.

While theology remains the bedrock, the most vocalized objections are, however, *biblical*. Here again the arguments are all too familiar. The injunction "you shall have no other Gods before me" is written into the very first commandment, with the warning "you shall not bow down to them or worship them; for I the Lord your God am a jealous God..." (Ex. 20:4ff.).

In responding to the Hindu-Buddhist context, this prohibition is reinforced by the many passages that prohibit the worship of idols and give explicit instructions to tear them down. As part of the process of settling down in the land of the Canaanites, the Israelites were asked to "destroy all their figured stones, destroy all their molten images and demolish all their high places" (Num. 33:52).

Few Christians take the trouble (because of the theological reason) to understand the meaning and significance of images in Hinduism and Buddhism. Nor do they pay attention to the use of images within the Roman Catholic tradition or to the use of icons in the Orthodox churches as "windows into God". For them the very presence of any image constitutes a turning away from the Lord God to the golden calf. This would be confirmed for them in the New Testament in such statements of Paul as: "... What fellowship is there between light and darkness? What agreement does Christ have with Belial? Or what does a believer share with an unbeliever?" (2 Cor. 6:14-16).

As often in such use of the Bible, the fact that there are other passages and themes that might help us to have more openness on this issue is ignored.

The biblical reasons, however, also run at a deeper level and relate to such concepts as "covenant", "election", "people of God", "revelation", "the one mediator", "no other name" and so on. The "missionary mandate" is seen as the decisive pointer to the gulf between Christians and others in such matters.

It is not difficult to collect a body of biblical passages and concepts that would militate against any thought of engaging in worship with peoples of other faith traditions.

The *liturgical* reason is perhaps the most immediate problem that a person who wants to participate in worship across religious traditions begins to experience. The word "liturgical" is used here in a special sense to denote the symbol system, rites, rituals, gestures and the structure, shape and form of worship that each religious community has evolved in the course of translating its faith into a sustained worship life, especially in community. Forms of worship in various religious traditions are very different and are not easily understood or entered into by those outside. Even the very concept of worship and the elements that go into it differ widely among religions.

The *cultural* reasons are very similar to the liturgical one. I know Christian friends from the West who would enter a Hindu temple at the height of the *puja*, when all the devotees are in a state of total rapture, and find the whole affair completely "chaotic"; some cannot imagine "worship" when the devotees are not seated in rows of pews listening to a preacher. Similarly there are Hindus who attend Christian services and find them no more than public lectures interspersed with prayers and hymns. Every time I entered a mosque at prayer time, even in Sri Lanka or India where I share with Muslims the general culture of the land, I had felt myself a "stranger" to the place. There is an "attitude of prayer" that is unique to the Islamic community and cannot be duplicated elsewhere or shared by those outside the fold.

The cultural dimension of a religion functions as a culture within a culture. Therefore, not only friends from the West but also Indian Christians have a hard time entering into the spirit of Hindu worship. This is not peculiar to the interfaith situation. I know Protestant friends who have, during ecumenical visits, attended Russian Orthodox or Greek Orthodox liturgical services and come out of them totally bewildered and even confused by their very richness.

For most Christians in the third world there is also a *psychological* block about participating in worship with other religious communities. First it has to do with the fact that many of these religious traditions are what they themselves or their ancestors had "left behind" to follow the "true faith" that was presented by the missionary or Christian evangelist. If they had believed that God listened to the prayer of the Hindu they might not have converted to Christianity. Second, one of the fears drilled into Christians, especially in the context of the predominance of other faiths, is the fear of compromise, of syncretism and the dilution of the Christian faith. Interfaith worship appears as a classic example of such compromise. And last, one faces the problem of identity. While Hindus, Muslims and Christians look alike and act in much the same way in their day-to-day life in society, their places of worship and the worship life itself give them particular identities as individuals and communities. There is something distinctive about the way each religious tradition has evolved in its worship life; its adherents see worship as one of the secure sources of identity, one they would like to retain and cherish.

It is interesting, in this context, to observe immigrant communities all over the world attempting to reproduce as much of their worship life as they possibly can in their new situations. The Buddhist population in a city in the United States, for example, may not be large, but still, despite the fact that they all follow Buddhism, the Thai, Vietnamese, Tibetan, Sri Lankan, Korean, Chinese, Cambodian and other versions of it are all reproduced in the city both in visible structures and in worship life. Some wonder why they spend so much of their scarce resources in building separate temples, especially when in new minority contexts an ecumenical expression of Buddhism would be far more desirable and viable. Separate structures, however, come up in city after city. This is not because they are anti-ecumenical; it is simply an issue of identity. Nor is it peculiar to Asians. When I first came to Geneva and wanted to worship in the English language, I had the chance to choose from among the Scottish, English or American cultural types!

A changing landscape

By the time I joined the WCC staff worship across religious barriers had already become an issue in quite a few member churches, especially in the Western hemisphere. Several factors have contributed to this development. The most important among them is the increased contact between Christians in the West and Buddhists, Hindus, Sikhs, Muslims and people of other faiths who had come to live among them as immigrants. Many who have had no immediate contact with these communities now had their first experience of them as praying, believing and worshipping communities with long spiritual histories. These religious traditions and some of their contemporary movements also engaged in missionary activities, offering alternatives to Christianity and secular humanism. Gradually all this led to a growing interest on the part of the younger generation of Christian "spiritual seekers" to try out meditation, yoga and the like as supplements to their Christian faith.

Today interfaith encounters, mixed marriages and the common search for peace during times of conflict give rise to situations where prayer or some form of worship is called for as part of the right response. The expectations on such occasions differ vastly, resulting in rather confused and even conflicting understandings of what is meant by "inter-religious prayer" or "inter-religious worship".

In a recent meeting jointly organized by the Office of Inter-religious Relations of the WCC and the Pontifical Council for Inter-religious Dialogue, Thomas Thangaraj gave what he called "five scenarios" that the phrase "inter-religious prayer" would bring to the mind of many Christians.[1]

First, some would consider the very presence of Christians in acts of worship of other traditions as a measure of participating in inter-religious prayer. For them presence includes involvement. Those who are opposed to inter-religious prayer are not likely to enter places of worship belonging to other traditions; even if they do, they will not remain there when an act of worship takes place. When the Dialogue Sub-unit held multilateral dialogue meetings, we would announce in advance which of the religious communities would be leading prayers each day. The prayers were held as the first event in the morning so that, while people of other traditions willing to be participants or to be present as observers could do so, others might join the meeting at the end of the prayers. This has nothing to do with over-sensitivity on the part of the organizers of the dialogue. Many would openly complain if they were "trapped" or "forced" into a situation of having to be present at other people's worship. They see this as an act of compromise. Therefore in all such meetings we would announce the options in advance: "To be involved to the extent the community leading the worship is able to invite us to participate", "to be silent observers", or "to be absent". We always had candidates for each of those options.

The *second* understanding of inter-religious prayer for many Christians is the use of rituals, gestures, readings and prayers from other religious traditions.

Some years ago I was asked to conduct a workshop on prayer. I gave the participants a few prayers and asked them to identify the authors and if possible the context of those prayers. One of them was the following:

> This is my prayer to thee, my Lord – Strike, strike at the root of penury in my heart. Give me the strength lightly to bear my joys and sorrows. Give me the strength to make my love fruitful in service. Give me the strength never to disown the poor. Or bend my knees before insolent might. Give me the strength to raise my mind high above daily trifles. And give me the strength to surrender my strength to thy will with love.[2]

Several participants thought that it was a prayer of St Francis of Assisi. Other responses included St Teresa of Avila, "a Christian saint" whose name they could not remember, Martin Luther, and "a verse from a hymn by Charles Wesley". The group was surprised to learn that it was from *Gitanjali* by the celebrated Hindu Bengali poet, Rabindranath Tagore.

It was interesting that none of them would attribute such a prayer to sources outside the Christian tradition, and of course there was no expectation that a prayer "belonging" to another religious tradition would be used in a Christian workshop on prayer.

If I used a prayer from the *Upanishads*, *Tiruvasagam* or a Sufi saint in the pulpit without identifying the source, there would be no adverse comment; and if there was a reaction it would be appreciative – "that was a beautiful prayer that you used today". But were I to identify the source of the prayer as Hinduism or Islam, that would provoke strong criticism among many parishioners, who would consider it an "inter-religious prayer"!

The *third* scenario is the normal one in inter-religious gatherings, consultations and national events where a multifaith group decides to have moments of prayer or is called upon to pray. The most widely reported instance in recent years was the call for a Day of Prayer for Peace at Assisi (1986) by Pope John Paul II. What happened there is along the model that has been in use in many interfaith gatherings, where the integrity of the worship tradition of each faith is respected, but the prayers are offered in the presence of other faith communities.

The *fourth* type has been a challenge to many teachers and chaplains of schools (in some parts of the world), hospitals and prisons, who are called to lead prayers at gatherings of people drawn from different faiths. Here a multifaith audience is already in place, or a context of openness may be taken for granted, and the leader's task is to design a mode and content of prayer that is both inclusive of and sensitive to the faiths of those present. Given the diversity of religious traditions and their approaches to worship, this has never been an easy task.

The *fifth* scenario is of more recent origin. Here people seek to go beyond the model of successive prayers in the presence of all to the possibility of "praying together". Several attempts have been made to prepare interfaith prayer services for persons from different religious traditions. The attempt in this area has been along two lines. The first is an attempt to include in one act of worship elements from different traditions. Thus, the invocation might come from Hinduism, a song from the Christian tradition, reading from the Quran, prayers from Sikhism and the blessings from Buddhism. The second involves the difficult task of producing new texts, prayers and songs that would be "acceptable" to all the groups participating in the worship.

The fifth scenario represents both the desired goal of interfaith worship and the intractable problems in attempting it. Those against inter-religious prayer have accused the first method within the fifth scenario as syncretistic and the second as going for the lowest common denominator, thus missing out on the central elements peculiar to each of the religions represented.

What then should we say? Is inter-religious worship or prayer a pointless pursuit that will in the end leave everyone dissatisfied? In spite of all the pressures of living, working and struggling together, should we decide that when it comes to praying we must maintain our separate identities and consider our ways and forms of worship as necessary and unchangeable? Will attempts at interfaith prayer eventually lead to the watering down of all our worship experiences?

The reluctance is of course understandable. And because of it many persons, especially in Christian leadership, participate in interfaith worship events with visible uncertainty and hesitation. I have watched Christian leaders participate in interfaith worship events; their body language conveys much more than what is said. Although some have gradually grown into it, many of them participate in interfaith worship with question marks written all over their faces! Some of them go up the stage much the same way children go to school for the first time. Many stand up there, alongside other religious leaders in full regalia, with a "when-will-this-thing-be-over?" expression, desperate to be backstage before any of their own congregation appear at the show. To any discerning person, some of the religious leaders at interfaith worship events appear to be there because of "diplomatic necessity" rather than any sense of conviction. Perhaps that is precisely what they would like to convey to their reluctant congregations, who might be wondering what in the world their bishop is doing up there with a Shinto priest, a Buddhist monk and a Hindu swami.

This is not just being frivolous. I have myself been a participant in many interfaith worship situations in all of the five scenarios described above, and have had the opportunity both to experience and observe first-hand what goes on. Part of the problem has to do with the different understandings within the religious communities on how much participation in another religious ritual is possible. In Japan, for example, it is common for a Buddhist to feel completely at home while participating in a Shinto or Christian worship event. While Christians are unwilling to share the consecrated elements with persons who are not part of their religious community, Hindus would, at the end of the *puja,* bring the *prasad* (food first offered to God during the *puja*) and offer it to all who are present at worship, and might even be offended if the hospitality is turned down.

When I was minister of the Methodist church in Jaffna, one of the staff of the overseas division of the Methodist Church in Britain came to visit the Jaffna church. One afternoon we decided to tour Jaffna. When we arrived at the Nallur Hindu temple, we noticed that the priest was performing a private *puja* for an extended family of about twenty persons. Our visitor wished to see what was going on, and we watched from a respectable distance. When the *puja* was over the priest offered the *prasad* to the family members, and seeing the European woman and me standing at some distance, began to approach us to offer it to us as well.

I could see my friend was in a state of panic. This was her first visit to a Hindu temple, she had told me, and I had not anticipated that it would lead to such an embarrassing situation. We had only moments to decide how to meet it, and no possibility of engaging in a theological discourse!

"You are free to turn it down," I whispered to her: "He will understand. I am receiving it because the issue here is hospitality, not food offered to idols."

I received in the traditional fashion and she followed, her hand slightly shaking.

We had a fascinating discussion later about the range of options available to us and what it might have meant for the person extending hospitality. As she boarded the train to go back to Colombo, she thanked me with a broad smile saying, "In Jaffna, you 'kill' people with your hospitality!" She must have meant the warmth of friendship and the lavish hospitality she was offered in many Jaffna homes. But somehow I could not help connecting it to the Hindu temple. There is hospitality, also in interfaith relations, that can be quite overwhelming.

While withdrawing to the comfort of our own worship world does appear to be the easiest option, even reluctant religious leaders are up there on the stage, even if only for diplomatic reasons, because we do have a new reality today that can no longer be ignored. As communities live in close proximity and face common issues and common problems, and share common visions for a just, reconciled and peaceful world, they come under enormous pressure also to pool their spiritual resources in dealing with them. In any case, in an increasingly multifaith world we constantly face situations that demand new initiatives and new ways of holding our faith in relationship to others. Isolationism, including in the religious and spiritual spheres, can be practised today only if we are prepared to opt out of society, or are willing to participate in it only on our own terms.

What then should we do?

Dimensions of the issue

In the work of the dialogue programme of the WCC we felt that the first and most important task in this area is to sort out the language and meanings given to words which create part of the confusion that prevails. In my own treatment of the subject so far in this chapter I have used the words "prayer" and "worship" interchangeably, only because they are in fact used in that way in many of the discussions and publications. The way forward lies in having greater clarity on what we mean by such words as "spirituality", "spiritual disciplines", "prayer", "worship", "liturgy" and so on, and on what is in fact called for, and not called for, in interfaith situations.

"Prayer" and "worship"

Anthropologists say that all human beings in all periods of history have had some practice of prayer. The urge to pray comes from their sense of the mystery that surrounds them in creation and of their own awareness of self-transcendence. It is said that even when more and more scientific explanations are found for the natural processes in creation, the miracle of life, its complexity and its purposefulness continue to fascinate human beings. So does the mystery of life and death, leading to the popular statement that human beings are incurably religious, even when they refuse to give it a label.

"Prayer" in this context is the attempt by human beings to be in communion or communication with the sacred, the holy, the Other, in common parlance, with God. In this respect "prayer", in the strict sense of the word, is the universal aspect of religion. "Prayer to religion", it is said, "is what rational thought is to philosophy." It is the language of the heart, the response to the miracle of life. Even though not all people necessarily engage in an active and conscious prayer life, it is an inalienable part of being human to have an "attitude" of prayer, especially when the human heart is elevated by the sense of the mystery of life or confronted with the reality of the finitude of life.

Human beings thus are "praying animals". When the very last bit of that true sense of prayer dies in them they turn into brutes, unleashing unimaginable suffering on other humans. It is not without significance that such acts are characterized as "brutal". Animal lovers today, however, are critical of our use of the word "brutal". They point out that in so far as animals generally follow the laws of nature, there are fewer "irrational killings" in the animal world. They would rather use the word "monstrous" to describe the acts of people who cannot or do not any longer pray. In other words, prayer is a "human" activity; the urge to pray is so universal that it transcends national, cultural and religious barriers.

"Worship", on the other hand, normally does not refer to a general quest, but to an ordered response to a realized experience of the Sacred within a specific religious community. It is significant that the word "worship" is generally used to refer not to acts of individuals but of communities. Here the emphasis is not on "search", "quest", "exploration" and so on, but on "praise", "thanksgiving", "adoration" and the "confession of faith". Every worshipping community has a "story" to tell. In worship, therefore, a community celebrates the central event that had been their "window" into the Divine. For the Jewish community it is the revelation of the

Torah on Mount Sinai, to the Muslims the revelation of the Quran, to the Christians the revelation in Jesus Christ, to the Hindu what the seers "saw" in the Vedas, and so on. Thus, worship is not an open-ended activity; it has points of reference; it is built on a story which is celebrated in myths, symbols, rites and rituals. Much of what happens in worship is meaningful only to those who share the "story".

A powerful illustration of this truth is recorded by David Brown, the late bishop of Guildford, England, when he writes about his relationship with Muslims:

> My distance from Islam came home to me in a sad but profound way one evening in Khartoum, when I went to the home of a Muslim leader. There were some thirty men sitting at ease in the courtyard and for an hour or more we enjoyed an open discussion about religious matters. Then the time came for the night prayer, and they formed ranks to say it together. I asked if I might stand with them, but the *Shaikh* told me I could not do so, since I did not have the right "intention" *(niyya)*. I had to remain standing at the edge of the courtyard. Even though I have walked on the approaches of Islam for over 30 years I can only speak of it as a stranger.[3]

The story is as moving as it is revealing. The Muslims are aware that the bishop has a full grasp of Islam and knows how to engage in Islamic prayer. They also know him as a person who had sympathetically accompanied Islam and Muslims for more than thirty years. Here they were not dealing with a "stranger" to them or to Islam. And still the bishop, in so far as he subscribes to the Christian "story", does not have the *niyya*, the right "intention", to be able to join the prayer line. To join that line, he has to be part of "their" story.

Thus even though the word "prayer" is used, the bishop was encountering Muslims at "worship". It is the "private space" of that religion where others would be out of place. I have also been in situations where Christian priests had to explain to Hindus attending Christian worship why they could not be invited to come forward and receive the eucharist.

Unfortunately, since much "prayer" takes place within the context of "worship" and some communities use the word "prayer" to indicate their "worship life", it is difficult to draw a hard and fast line between the two. There is, however, a growing awareness of the need to make the distinctions between what is "internal" to the life of a religious community and where the community can be open to others both in the extending and accepting of invitations to pray together. Many Christians today are looking for clear guidance on this issue.

Pastoral dimension

The issue of inter-religious prayer thus is no longer a privileged question engaging the attention of specialized groups engaged in interfaith explorations. The pastoral dimension of the issue is what has concerned the WCC's Office on Inter-religious Relations and the Holy See's Pontifical Council for Inter-religious Dialogue.

Together they started in 1994 a four-year joint reflection and study of the issue, beginning first to document what has been happening in the churches, collecting worship materials and guidelines that were being used, and calling on those engaged in interfaith prayer to recount their experiences.

This was followed by two events in Bangalore, India, and Bose, Italy, where practitioners of interfaith prayer, biblical scholars and theologians sought to open up the issues involved and to show directions in which they might be followed up in the future.[4]

The Bangalore statement puts forward the pastoral dimension as the key issue:

Participation in inter-religious prayer is not an optional activity restricted to an elite group, but an urgent call for a growing number of Christians today, and should be a matter of concern for all Christians. In the pluralistic world in which we live, concrete situations of everyday life provide opportunities for encounters with people of living faiths. These include interfaith marriages, personal friendship, praying together for common causes (in the context of war, racism, human rights violations,

AIDS, etc.), national holidays, religious festivals, school assemblies, meetings between monastic communities of different faiths and gatherings at interfaith dialogue centres. Sometimes, it is prayer for a common purpose, perhaps in a crisis situation, which draws people of different faiths to pray together. Often, the experience of working together on a social project leads to a desire to pray together. In all these contexts, respect, honesty, transparency and openness nurture inter-religious prayer and make it possible.[5]

I have quoted the above to emphasize that the question "Can we pray together?" is not an academic one; it will become more and more important in the future to all who believe in prayer. In Bangalore, the searching of the scriptures showed that in the Bible there are passages that appear to be against such prayer, and yet others that present God as the compassionate one who listens to the cry of every human heart. The Bible affirms the particularity of the call of a people to a specific faith and discipleship; yet, it stresses God's intention to bring all things to fulfilment.

Having weighed the context of the churches and the witness of the scriptures, the Bangalore statement had this to say in conclusion:

While recognizing that the development of inter-religious prayer will be related to particular situations, we see a great value in the World Council of Churches Office on Inter-religious Relations and the Pontifical Council for Inter-religious Dialogue continuing to provide opportunities to share and reflect on this experience, so that churches together joyfully respond to the new opportunities of not only meeting and working with members of other religions, but also, where appropriate, praying with them. Such prayer, we believe, is a symbol of hope, which both reminds us of God's purpose and promise for justice and peace for all people and calls us to offer ourselves to be used in this work.[6]

The meeting at Bose, a year later, went deeper into the theological issue and of the different kinds of situations of prayer that call for different approaches. The Bose statement too affirmed the importance of the issue to churches and other religious communities:

As prayer transforms our life, so inter-religious prayer should have a positive impact on the life and relationship of our communities. As we move into deeper encounters in inter-religious prayer, we might experience it as a journey, realizing that prayer in itself is open-ended, a sign into the mystery of God.[7]

Spirituality and spiritual disciplines

My own exploration of this subject within the WCC, however, did not begin with the question of inter-religious prayer, but with the issue of "spirituality". Following the Vancouver assembly of the WCC (1983), the WCC's programme on Renewal and Congregational Life began exploring the concern for "a spirituality for our times". The word "spirituality" was a rather vague notion, and soon there was awareness among those dealing with the issue of the widespread use of the word among people of other religious traditions. Of even more interest was the realization that in recent times many of the persons within the church who had chosen to undertake a "spiritual journey" or wanted to explore the "spiritual dimension of life" had opted for "spiritual disciplines" or "spiritual practices" that they had discovered from within other religious traditions. It was interesting to discover, for example, that even though meditation had been part of the church's tradition, many Christians were looking to Buddhist or Hindu meditation techniques to centre their life in God.

The more we probed, the more we discovered that there had been an inter-religious "dialogue of spirituality" that had not received the attention of the church or even of those concerned with dialogue.

Ann E. Chester, in an essay on "Zen and Me", says that she had to turn to Buddhism for help because of the over-emphasis within Christianity on the spoken word, which in her view tends to limit God to the meaning of the words spoken.

But "centring down", as the Quakers put it, remaining at the "still point" within, completely open to the all-pervading energy of God, was to be in touch with myself, with who I really am; it is also to give God full freedom to help me become what I am capable of being... Zazen has helped me to seek that depth, to be at home there, to deepen it, to act out of it.[8]

What has been the story within the church of spiritual journeys that had been helped by spiritual practices originating from other religious traditions? What has been the experience of those who have undertaken that journey for long periods of time?

In December 1987 the Dialogue programme, in collaboration with the programme on Renewal and Congregational Life, brought together about twenty persons (in Kyoto, Japan) from the Orthodox, Roman Catholic and Protestant traditions who had spent at least ten years of their lives engaged in spiritual practices from other religious traditions. The group also included persons who, while practising such disciplines, were engaged with others in the struggles for justice and peace.

The stories they shared were fascinating. Some have been drawn to use other spiritual disciplines because, living in proximity to others (as in Asia), they were impressed by the visible manifestation of authentic spiritual life in them. Others were attracted by the cultural affinity and roots of the spiritual practices of other traditions, such as the kind of music, art, gestures, rites and meditative practices that constituted their spiritual discipline. Many from the West were motivated in their spiritual journey "by a sense that there was 'something missing' in the spiritual life of our churches, a shallowness or emptiness, or a lack of deepening guidance". They said that especially in the Hindu and Buddhist traditions they found "forms of practice and prayer that have been both challenging and enriching".[9]

As the result of intense sharing of such experiences of benefits, problems, risks and possibilities of venturing into the spiritual practices of other traditions, the group was able to make these three affirmations in its final statement:

> First, we affirm the great value of dialogue at the level of spirituality in coming to know and understand people of other

faiths as people of prayer and spiritual practice, as seekers and pilgrims with us, and as partners with us in working for peace and justice.

Second, we affirm the deepening of our own Christian faith in the journeys that have taken us into the spiritual life and practice of other faiths. In walking along with the other, with the stranger, like the disciples on the road to Emmaus, we have had, in our sharing, the experience of recognition. We have seen the unexpected Christ and have been renewed.

Third, we affirm the work of the Spirit in ways that move beyond the Christian compound and across the frontiers of religion and take us into creative involvement with people of other faiths in the struggles of the world.[10]

Even though this meeting brought together persons who have had long experience in this field and have become experts in the art of integrating, practising and expressing deep Christian convictions through spiritual practices from other faiths, the issue itself is of immediate interest to many Christians in their day-to-day life.

Is it all right to meditate using Buddhist guidance on meditation? Can I practice yoga and still be a Christian? Is it permissible to read other scriptures and spiritual writings, and will they contribute to my spiritual development?

Ultimately such questions are about the self-sufficiency of our own traditions. They raise the question whether there are areas in which the spiritual life and practices of our own traditions can be corrected, enriched and enhanced by interaction with others.

When I was a student and was used only to Methodist worship, I was under the impression that this was the most adequate form of Christian worship. At college, out of necessity, I worshipped according to the Anglican tradition and came to a new understanding of liturgy, and to appreciate the strengths and weaknesses of both forms of worship. In the ecumenical movement I have encountered many other forms, ranging from Quaker meetings to the Eastern and Oriental Orthodox liturgies, which opened even more windows into the manifold ways in which a community might celebrate its faith.

In 1983 I was secretary for worship at the WCC Vancouver assembly. The most important issue we raised at the first meeting of the assembly worship committee was this: The people who come together for worship, around three thousand of them, are from different cultures, speak different languages, sing different songs and come from different confessions with different styles of worship. Should we see this as a problem or as an opportunity? Should we try to overcome the diversity or use it creatively?

That one consideration made all the difference to the assembly's worship life, and the worship at Vancouver became a landmark in ecumenical worship, which has been one of the most memorable dimensions of ecumenical life in recent decades.

Why did the Vancouver worship experience become so meaningful and exciting to so many of the participants?

The reasons are many, the most obvious among them being the simple fact that every confession represented at the assembly experienced its own tradition enriched and enhanced by the way the riches of different traditions and cultures were forged together into acts of worship. People were able to enter into a "fuller" dimension of worship than they had experienced within their own tradition. They also became convinced that they had much more to learn about worship itself.

A personal experience

This truth had already come home to me, at the level of an interfaith encounter, through an interesting episode to which I have returned often, mainly to illustrate the meaning of dialogue.

It too happened in Colombo.

Once while I was walking along the main street (Galle Road) I met one of the Hindu friends that Retnanantham had introduced to me. It was late on a Friday afternoon and we were passing the Hindu temple at Bambalapitiya.

The Hindu friend asked me if I could wait for five minutes while he went into the temple to worship. I agreed, and stayed outside looking at the magazines displayed at the tobacconist near the entrance to the temple. My friend was back in five minutes to continue the conversation we had begun.

Some time later I had to write a paper on Hindu worship and decided to look more closely at what happened in the Hindu temple. Several things struck me that I had not noticed before.

As one enters the temple at the time of the *puja,* the first thing one experiences is the special aroma from the camphor and incense that are being burned in front of the deity. Then, one's eyes are filled with religious sculpture and paintings, the image beautifully clothed and garlanded, and the *arathi,* the lamp that is raised in front of the image several times in circular motions, both as a mark of respect and as the prayer of invocation. The ears are filled with the sounds of the chanting of the *mantra,* the ringing of the bells and the beating of the drums. Now the priest brings to those gathered the *prasad* from the altar (a mixture of milk, water and fruit), and having received it, and having "seen" and "been seen" by the deity *(darshan),* one prostrates oneself on the ground and rises again, invoking the name of the deity representing God at that temple: *"Siva, Siva!", "Om Muruga", "Om Sakthi", "Govinda"* and so on. Once this brief act of worship is over, the devotee is free to leave.

I realized that through three thousand years of experimentation Hindus have developed a special "strategy" of catering to all the senses in an act of worship – of smell, sight, hearing, taste and touch – all at once and with much intensity, to help the devotee "to rise to the awareness of standing in the presence of God". If worship has to do primarily with standing in the presence of God, of *dharsana* or seeing and being seen by God, there was no need to tarry much longer. Little wonder that my Hindu friend was able to complete the worship in five minutes.

A surprise awaited me when I shared this with the Hindu friend. Impressed with what I had to say about Hindu worship, he asked if he could come to one of my Sunday services. His contact with Christian worship had not gone beyond school assemblies.

Of course I had to extend to him an invitation to my church at Moor Road at 6:00 the following Sunday where I was to lead the worship and preach. But I was nervous, especially after my "discovery" of the multifaceted nature of Hindu worship catering to all the senses all at once.

At Moor Road church we had a little wooden cross standing on the bare altar table and a vase of flowers. Then there were of course rows and rows of pews. Apart from that, there was nothing to "see", to "smell", to "taste" or to "touch".

I suddenly realized that we Methodists have put all our eggs in the one basket of "hearing". Prayers, hymns, readings, sermons – all cater to the one sense of "hearing".

Little wonder, I told myself, that while the Hindu can worship in five minutes, we must take an hour or more, and that on each occasion the sermon must make up for all that is lacking, in order to enable those present to "rise to the awareness of standing in the presence of God".

Well, we may have got used to the "hymn sandwich" (hymn – prayer – hymn – readings – hymn – sermon – hymn), but will a Hindu be satisfied with "one-sense" worship?

On Sunday I stuck to the traditional pattern with the usual "stirring" sermon. I saw my Hindu friend seated in the last row. At the end of the service I went around greeting the people, and when I came to my Hindu friend, to my surprise he was deeply excited. It had been a wonderful experience for him. We decided to meet to talk about it.

"So what was so wonderful about the worship?", I asked him the next day, wondering if he was being "nice" to me, as we say in Sri Lanka.

No, he was not being "nice" to me. "You have been to our temple," he said, "and you have seen how we come and go during the *puja*. There is no common intention; we all stand there as individuals. But in the church there were some three hundred people all seated quietly with the same intention to pray. And then," he continued, "in the temple we do not read the scripture, the priest does not explain the scripture and apply it to life."

I remembered that in the Hindu tradition teaching and priestly ministries are usually separated. The priest does not teach; he performs the rituals. There is no teaching done with the *puja*. Teaching, when it happens, takes place outside the worship context.

He was also impressed with the intercession, how we remembered members in need by name, how we prayed for peace, justice and so on. It had altogether been a spiritually enriching experience for him. Obviously his other senses had not been complaining!

But this was a revealing experience for me. Here was I, a Methodist minister, going into a Hindu temple and discovering dimensions of worship long lost to the Methodist tradition. And here is a Hindu, coming into a Methodist worship to discover dimensions of worship missing in his worship experience.

I often recall this experience when we talk about dialogue in general to illustrate how dialogue leads to mutual correction, mutual enrichment and mutually helpful self-criticism. I also use it to stress the point that Diana Eck, moderator of the WCC Sub-unit on Dialogue, used to make: "We not only need to know the others; we also need the others to know ourselves."

It is no wonder that most people who have ventured into other spiritual traditions have found their own faith enriched, and those who are involved with other faiths see interfaith worship as something that the churches should take with greater seriousness as they look towards the future.

Looking to the future

For reasons given in the earlier part of this chapter, interfaith worship will continue to be a difficult and controversial issue in the life of the churches. As with the issue of mission, so also with the question of interfaith worship, real change can come only with a more radical reassessment and restatement of the Christian faith for a pluralistic world.

In the meantime, it appears to me that the developments on the ground demand a new approach to worship within all religious traditions. What might be possible and necessary can be represented in three concentric circles, as P.D. Devanandan did when he spoke of creed, cultus and culture, when dealing with the indigenization of the faith.

The inner circle represents the core of liturgical life in which each community celebrates its "story". This in Christian tradition, for example, is the celebration of the eucharist, in which meaningful participation is linked to what Christians believe God to have done through the life, death and resurrection of Jesus Christ. This is the religious community's "private space", providing it with distinctive identity and cohesion as a community gathered in celebration. A community may decide to be "hospitable", to allow others to be observers in this space, to maintain an unobtrusive presence, to participate to the extent that the community is able to invite them, and to be open to the witness that the community gives to their faith through the celebration of the "story" that is formative.

Beyond this, and sharing the same centre, should be a second circle, which might be called the community's participation in a "commonwealth of spirituality". It is indeed unfortunate that most religious communities, especially at the official level, are reluctant even to "touch" the best spiritual resources and practices available, if they are known to have originated outside their own tradition. Much of this attitude is due to prejudice rather than considered theological reflection. As mentioned earlier, as a pastor I was able to use any number of resources from other religious traditions in a Christian service provided I did not in any way reveal their source. If, however, I were to mention where they are from, all the defences would be up.

The group that met in Kyoto to discuss spirituality in interfaith dialogue witnessed to the fact that it is indeed possible to use other spiritual practices, scriptures, written and symbolic resources to enlarge one's spiritual vistas and to deepen one's religious life. It was significant that they did not feel they were being syncretistic, because all the resources they had acquired from Buddhism, Hinduism, Islam and so on, in their experience, enabled them to deepen their own core faith, and also helped them to discover new dimensions of spiritual life and practice.

This has relevance also to the gospel and culture debate. The Kyoto group did not begin with a clear distinction between gospel and culture, and then present the issue as a "problematic" and ask, "And how are we going to relate these two?" That kind of approach has plagued ecumenical discussions from the beginning. It makes the assumption that there is a "gospel" that is culture-free, and "culture" that can be extricated from what it expresses. Since the gospel is about incarnation it can only exist as expressed within a culture, and any encounter of its challenge can only happen from within some culture. The question then is, "Now that I have responded to the challenge of the gospel, how can that find expression in my life? How can I 'be rooted and grounded in love' and have 'the power to comprehend the breadth and the length and the height and the depth' and 'to know the love of Christ that surpasses knowledge' and so 'be filled with all the fullness of God'" (Eph. 3:17-19)?

No spiritual resource or practice needs to be "out of bounds" in the exploration and expression of that love simply because it originated outside one's own tradition. I have myself been deeply moved by the depth of devotion and the enormous sense of the overwhelming grace of God that is witnessed to in the Hindu scriptures like *Tevaram, Tiruvasagam,* and the penetrating ethical-moral analysis and guidance given in the *Tirukkural.* I have had no difficulty turning to them often, as I turn to the Bible. The fact that these Hindu scriptures name the One beyond all names as "Sivan" has never bothered me. Syncretism is not innately present in other resources, as many seem to imply. Syncretism has to do with what one does with these resources and what one does with one's own faith in embracing them. Religions are not fortresses to be defended; they are springs for the nourishment of human life.

While most religious communities, certainly at the official level, are still very nervous about moving in that direction, the barriers to such spiritual practices are constantly being breached by the younger generation in its search for an authentic spirituality. There is a need to lower all barriers so that the spiritual resources of all religious traditions will become the common property of all.

Some would have great difficulty with this suggestion because they believe that what happens in the second circle would be truly authentic for any religious community only when it flows out of and is an expression of the faith at the core. Otherwise, they would argue, the result is eclecticism, a curious, confused and unproductive amalgam of "practices" rooted in nothing except the practice itself. Then there are also practices in all religions that are considered to be superstitious, or contrary to fundamental values upheld by one or another of the religious traditions. In KKS, while I used to be deeply impressed by the *thevarams* sung at our neighbour's house, I was put off by the animal sacrifices offered at the *Mariamman* temple some distance from home – another dimension of religious expression that passes as Hinduism. Not all practices are "spiritual" simply because they are "religious".

These considerations have been at the heart of the traditional objection to openness to the spiritual practices of other religions. The Kyoto group, however, felt that this is a theoretical issue, raised mainly by those who have not undertaken such spiritual journeys. As in everything else, in spiritual practices too there is need for discernment, discrimination and rejection. What we are faced with, in the traditional approach, is an indiscriminate fear of anything that is not "ours".

For the Kyoto group, such fear appeared empty because they found that the practices they had adopted only deepened their awareness, commitment and rootedness to the centre. They also found that, without that freedom to explore, they were confined to a narrow understanding of the centre, defined within some culture in some period of history. In fact genuinely indigenous and contextual theologies can arise only within that space of freedom and exploration. Otherwise indigenous theologies may continue to look like vases of flowers plucked from the neighbours' gardens, rather than the flowering plants that draw nourishment from the different soils in which the gospel is planted.

There will of course be eclecticism, the irresponsible and unproductive amalgam of practices merely to satisfy one's curiosity. There could be expressions of religious life that not only stray from but even betray the core faith. But these do not happen only when one moves beyond one's tradition to explore spirituality. False religion, ceremonial religion, betrayal, syncretism and apostasy are prevalent internally in all religions. Most often it is not what goes in from the outside but what comes from the inside that defiles us. Otherwise why would we need prophets? And "heresies" are important for the life of the church. They arise only in periods in the history of a religion when there is genuine, but bold and daring, reflection on the meaning of the faith, and when concerted attempts are made to enter into a critical dialogue with the culture and the context in which the faith community lives. Genuine "orthodoxy" can only emerge out of "genuine heresies".

We cannot refrain from venturing for the kingdom out of our fear to take risks. We cannot say to the Householder when he returns, "Master, we (I) knew that you were a harsh man, reaping where you did not sow, and gathering where you did not scatter seed; so we (I) were afraid, and went and hid the talent in the ground. Here is what is yours" (Matt. 25:24-25).

The kingdom of God is more daring than that. It is based on the belief that while some seeds will inevitably fall along the path where birds eat them up, on rocky ground where they cannot grow, and among thorns that choke them, there will indeed be a harvest – thirty, sixty and a hundred fold! The birds, rocks and thorns are no reason to stop sowing. Sowing must continue. Without sowing there can be no reaping.

Then comes the third concentric circle, worship in the interfaith context. As we have seen, it has become impossible for religious communities to live in isolation from one another. More importantly, there is a gathering recognition that if religion is to make any impact on the world we live in, religions must cooperate among themselves and bring their efforts and voices together in addressing issues. It is this realization that has resulted in the proliferation of interfaith organizations nationally and globally, and in the emergence of issue-oriented interfaith groups. The strengthening of the interfaith movement is also seen in the intention to hold the Parliament of World's Religions on a more regular basis, in the attempt to set up United Religions to accompany the United Nations, and in such efforts as the drawing up of a global ethic and religious charter to fight discrimination, intolerance and all that leads to genocide. All these developments have brought even more pressure on the issue of interfaith worship and prayer. But religious communities, while acting together on a good many issues, are unable to pray together because their "stories" do not match.

The third circle should address this problem.

Each community has its own "narrative" that defines it. That narrative, as seen earlier, is important to its life, identity and worship. It is the defining narrative of that specific community. And it is only natural that we have such independent narratives as individual religious communities, for all religions evolved either in isolation from others or as reform movements within existing religions needing to have identity in difference. Many of the interfaith efforts over the past decades were meant to promote conversation among these separate narratives and to enable them to respect and give space to each other.

But as communities grow even closer together, there is also the need to create "meta"-narratives that serve the "human story" and the common destiny that is ours as a global community. To go back to KKS, I had no narrative within the religious sphere to make sense of my neighbours as religious persons except, of course, as objects of conversion. At that time I did not know what the problem was. Now I realize that my narrative was too narrow to make sense of the outside world (except in mission) because in it there was no place for any other narratives.

I have studied the great Indian epics *Ramayana* and *Mahabharata*. What is fascinating about them, among other things, is that there are numerous stories within the one Story. Any one of those "stories within the Story" would stand on its own, and convey a penetrating insight into human nature or provide an important ethical insight. At the same time they are within the one Story and are essential both to the development of the plot and to the total impact the epic is meant to make on the hearers or readers.

Each religion of course has a kind of meta-narrative of its own (like creation – fall – consummation) to situate its core narrative. The problem is that there is no place in them for other stories. The Human Story is of epic proportions. A single story, in which there is no room for any other, cannot do justice to it. If the story is of epic proportions, we need nothing less than an epic on it.

This is not a plea to work towards a universal religion of humankind, or a "call to unite all religions" under some vague ethical or religious notions. One of my tasks at the WCC dialogue desk has been to respond to documents sent to the WCC by people who have found the "Solution to Unite Mankind [sic] under One Religion", "Proposals for Uniting the Abrahamic Faiths", "Proposals for the Spiritual Unity of Humanity" and so on. When these arrived, addressed to the WCC, colleagues in the General Secretariat simply put the stamp "For suitable action" or "Please reply" and sent them to the Dialogue sub-unit.

Many of them are the result of reflection and hard work that individuals have put in over several years. Most of them also reveal painstaking research, documentation and sifting of facts and figures on what is happening to religion and religious communities around the world. Often they also show an awareness of the contents of the different faith traditions. Though some of the suggestions are frivolous and naive, a number of them are sincere and serious proposals made by persons who are deeply convinced that the divided and at times conflictual relationship among religious communities do much harm to human life. They often reveal real spiritual concern over the divisions based on religion, and a conviction of the enormous potential religions have for the healing of the world, if only we could harness their spiritual energies.

The WCC of course is committed to promoting unity among people of a single religious tradition. It was formed as an expression of the unity of the churches and "to prepare the way for a much fuller and much deeper expression of that unity". That process of preparation has gone on for many years. If realism is any virtue, we had it in good measure!

Interfaith organizations such as the World Conference on Religion and Peace (WCRP) and United Religions Initiatives and all interfaith dialogue programmes seek to bring religious traditions closer together in order to promote understanding and cooperation among them. These are important initiatives and have borne much fruit. But proposals to establish a "common religion for humankind", or to bring "all religions together into unity" are far more problematic. There is at present no mechanism to implement such proposals. They also fail to take serious account of the non-theological and non-spiritual factors that are at the centre of much of our divisions.

Meta-narrative evolves out of the life of the community. The systematization should follow, not precede, experience. Therefore, one can only say that the Story that includes the stories is in its initial stage of evolution. The "proposals" that we receive are not products but the signs that this meta-narrative is "in the making", and that we are in a process where all our independent narratives are being brought together into an epic.

It is little wonder, then, that despite all the difficulties we face in reconciling our stories and our symbol systems, we do have interfaith worship occasions, and interfaith prayer materials and multifaith service orders are being produced. Such prayer/worship is no longer held in secret, hidden from the eyes of officialdom, but in cathedrals, on highly visible national occasions, on TV – and in Assisi. Some of them are led by the heads of religious communities who would, in a theological context, have few or no tools to explain what they are doing! Without a meta-narrative, what they do makes no sense. Inadequate as such acts are, they nevertheless contribute to the evolution of that narrative.

In the third concentric circle, then, we are in the unfamiliar territory of interfaith prayer and worship. On many occasions we are called upon to pray, and especially when a calamity befalls a community we dare not refuse to pray together. It will be ambiguous; it will appear to be compromising; it may not fully satisfy any of us in the group; but as praying people, we dare not refuse to pray.

Our need to learn to pray together, however, is not just a matter of expediency, resulting from religious communities increasingly being thrown together because of population movements. Those studying the development of the religious life of humankind are convinced that as a human community we are on the threshold of a new "critical corporate consciousness" of being a global community. Wilfred Cantwell Smith, for example, is convinced that the gradual convergence of different religious communities has now reached the period of "a common religious history" of humankind. There was a time, Smith says, when we could speak of a Christian, Islamic or Hindu religious history, but now they are all becoming "strands" in a total human religious history, for now we are being pushed to a stage in which every religious person has been opened to the possibility of learning from all the religious traditions.[11]

As the boundaries that strictly and radically separate religious communities begin to weaken gradually, as did denominational boundaries during recent decades, we are entering, even as we enter a new century and a new millennium, a new religious reality of an uncharted territory. In the third concentric circle of our prayer life, then, we are in the wilderness, looking for a new formation, a new sense of who God is, and a new discovery of who we are *all together* as God's people. For, as St Paul says, we know "that the creation itself will be set free from its bondage to decay and will obtain the freedom of the glory of the children of God" and that "the whole creation has been groaning in labour pains until now", even as "we ourselves, who have the first fruit of the Spirit, groan inwardly while we wait for adoption, the redeeming of our bodies".

It is in this context of attempting to link the narrative of the redemption of the Christians in Rome (to whom Paul was writing the letter) to the meta-narrative of cosmic redemption that Paul also confesses that "we do not know how to pray as we ought". Then come the words of encouragement: that the Spirit intercedes "with sighs too deep for words", and that "God, who searches the heart, knows what is the mind of the Spirit, because the Spirit intercedes for the saints according to the will of God" (Rom. 8:18-27).

We are where the first disciples were when they were faced with a new reality. Although they were of a community that had prayed for centuries, they went to Jesus and asked, "Lord, teach us to pray." The challenge of praying with others can be no less demanding.

The three concentric circles, in the spiritual experience of believers, will be closely inter-related. Believers will also find that they influence one another in all directions.

"Can we pray together?" we asked. It appears that we need to pray our way through to find an answer. This might have been what the group that met on inter-religious prayer in Bose meant in the words that we have quoted above:

> As we move into deeper encounters in inter-religious prayer, we might experience it as a journey, realizing that prayer itself is open-ended, a sign into the mystery of God.[12]

NOTES

[1] M. Thomas Thangaraj, "A Theological Reflection on the Experience of Inter-religious Prayer", in the report of a consultation on inter-religious prayer, *Pro Dialogo/Current Dialogue,* bulletin 98, 1998, 2, pp.186-88.

58

2 Rabindranath Tagore, *Gitanjali* (song offerings), London, Macmillan & Co., 1996, song 36, p.28.

3 David Brown, "Meeting Muslims", in *The Churches and Islam in Europe (II)*, Geneva, 1982, pp.47-48. Quoted in *Can We Pray Together? Guidelines on Worship in a Multi-Faith Society*, London, British Council of Churches/Committee for Relations with People of Other Faiths, London, 1983, p.1.

4 Inter-religious Prayer, *Pro Dialogue/ Current Dialogue* (joint number), bulletin 98, 1998, 2. This gives the history of the project, the key presentations made and three evaluations from Roman Catholic, Orthodox and Protestant perspectives. For the statements from the Bangalore and Bose meetings see pp.231-43.

5 *Ibid.*, p.231.

6 *Ibid.*, p.236.

7 *Ibid.*, p.243.

8 Ann E. Chester, "Zen and Me", *Spring Wind*, IV, no. 4, winter 1984-85, pp.25-26.

9 Tosh Arai and Wesley Ariarajah, eds, *Spirituality in Interfaith Dialogue*, Geneva, WCC, 1989, p.1.

10 *Ibid.*, p.1-2.

11 W.C. Smith, *Towards a World Theology*, London, Macmillan, 1981. See esp. his chapters on "A History of Religions in the Singular" and "Religious Life as Participation in a Process".

12 *Op. cit.*, p.243.

4. Women and Dialogue:
Is Dialogue Compromised?

In November 1995 I was invited to the Irish School of Ecumenics in Dublin, Ireland, for a conference on "Pluralism and the Religions: The Theological and Political Dimensions", to present a paper on "The Impact of Inter-religious Dialogue on the Ecumenical Movement". I learned a lot from the papers presented at the conference. One of them, which I remember vividly, was given by Ursula King, professor in the department of theology and religious studies at the University of Bristol, England. The title of her paper was "Feminism: The Missing Dimension in the Dialogue of Religions".

Full and equal participation of women in church and society has been one of the long-standing commitments of the WCC, meant also to apply to WCC's own structures and programmes. While the commitment is clear and decisive, its implementation in its programmatic life has, for a variety of reasons, been somewhat uneven. Within the dialogue programme of the WCC too we have had, and still have, some very effective women's participation, but the overall record remains poor.

Diana Eck of Harvard University was for many years the moderator of the sub-unit's working group. She not only gave outstanding leadership, but was also one of the most effective spokespersons and promoters of the concern in the churches and academic institutions during the most critical years of WCC's dialogue work. In her report to the meeting of the Working Group in Casablanca, Morocco, in June 1989, she pointed out how glaring the absence of women was in interfaith events and efforts:

> We have strained over the years to involve women in dialogue, but frankly we have not done very well. There have been many international interfaith initiatives in the last few years. The most published are those that involve "religious leaders" brought together at the Assisi Day of Prayer called by Pope John Paul II, or the Oxford Global Forum of religious leaders and parliamentarians. Such events provide a heightened consciousness of the fact of our inter-religious relations, and our interdependence. But they have also served to underscore in a dramatic

and a shameful way what is missing in international and inter-religious affairs today – the voices and faces of women. The glossy photographs of the Assisi and Oxford events show the resplendent diversity of swamis and rabbis, archbishops and imams, the Dalai Lama and the archbishop of Canterbury. Our WCC meetings have not had a better record of including women: in Ajaltoun, Lebanon (March 1970), two of the 38 participants were women; in Broumana, Lebanon (July 1972), one of the 46 participants was a woman; in Colombo, Sri Lanka (April 1974), five of the 54 were women; in Mauritius (January 1983), ten of the 32 were women; in New Delhi (November 1987), nine of the 41 who actually attended were women, although 16 women were among the 61 invited.[1]

Thus, although there had been a consciousness of the issue and efforts to address it, the dialogue programme has suffered from insufficient involvement of women and the absence of women's concerns in the issues taken up for dialogue.

The problem was even more acute in the case of our dialogue partners. On the one hand, we wanted them also to involve more women on their side; on the other, the partners were sensitive to the issue of "demanding" or "dictating" the nature of the composition of their side. Over a period of time, however, our Jewish, Muslim, Hindu and Buddhist partners began to accept that in their dialogues within the WCC context there would be at least some women on both sides. But here, too, the participation of women remained more symbolic than real because men would set both the agenda and the framework of the discussion.

Ursula King's paper on the "missing dimension", therefore, was an important reminder in a conference of 130 participants. It showed how inadequate and tentative even the WCC's efforts have been, and that the whole dialogue enterprise was marked by the absence of women and women's issues. It also meant that the issue of "dialogue" was absent in much of the radical rethinking going on among women.

King's criticism was forthright:

Inter-religious dialogue, as currently understood, practised and promoted in many parts of the world, particularly among Christians, is strongly marked by the absence of women. Nor have feminist writers on religion, when critiquing the patriarchal framework of different religions, paid much attention to the new developments in inter-religious dialogue circles. If one examines current inter-religious activities, personnel and publications from a critical gender perspective, it is evident that, apart from a few, rare exceptions, feminism remains the missing dimension of dialogue. This could be substantiated by reference to numerous examples, such as the official dialogue activities of the World Council of Churches or those of the Vatican, or those of a new foundation such as the International Interfaith Centre in Oxford, England, or the various centennial celebrations of the 1893 World's Parliament of Religions organized in Bangalore, Chicago and other places in 1993. Gender considerations are usually never an integral part of such organizations and events.[2]

In her paper King goes beyond this criticism to offer creative ideas on "the challenge of feminism for inter-religious dialogue" and of "the challenge of interfaith dialogue to feminism", drawing from them the "challenge of women's dialogue to structures and institutions concerned with inter-religious dialogue".[3]

I agreed with her partly because I have had first-hand experience of how creative a dialogue among women of different religious traditions can be, both in fostering relationships and in bringing up issues on and about "religion" itself that never surface in a dialogue among men.

In June 1988 Diana Eck and I worked together to facilitate a gathering in Toronto of some fifty women from eight different religious traditions. It was sponsored by the Dialogue sub-unit in collaboration with the WCC sub-unit on Women in Church and Society. I was the only man in the group, providing the logistical support for the meeting with the assistance of the local planning group. For seven days, all through the organized part of the dialogue, I was on a "silent retreat" of listening and learning, which was in itself an important discipline for me, quite a change from my normal practice of talking too often at meetings and dialogues. It also gave me an opportunity to observe some of the distinctive features that characterize a dialogue among women.

The first was the speed with which the group bonded, despite the fact that no previous inter-religious meeting organized by the Dialogue sub-unit had brought together such a diversity of traditions. In addition to Christians, Jews, Muslims, Hindus and Buddhists, representing their great internal diversity, there were women from the Bahai community in Toronto, two women from the Native American tradition of Chippewa Cree from the Rocky Bay Reservation in Montana, a Mescalero Apache, and two from the Wiccan tradition of Goddess spirituality, a tradition seen by many as representing the "spiritual wing" among women of the "environmental movement". In a meeting of men, the very composition of such a group might have become rather controversial. But here on the very first day the group had bonded, and by the second day a common "we" and "us women" had begun to emerge.

We had included in the group several outstanding scholars of religion so that they would be able to speak about their respective religious traditions with scholarly authority and informed understanding of the historical development of their traditions. The second factor that struck me was their remarkable lack of any dogmatic approach in representing their traditions. While most men approach and appropriate their religious tradition primarily as an intellectual and dogmatic deposit that has become part of their understanding of life and reality, women appeared to have a more nuanced understanding of religion. While many of the women made excellent contributions on the content of their religion in scripture and tradition, there was little defensiveness and a complete lack of dogmatism.

The third feature was the readiness to share experiences and stories, both from their personal lives and from their community's spiritual journey, which no doubt, helped in their growing together into a community within a short period. Most men, especially in leadership positions in their religious communities, would rarely share their personal background, much less the spiritual struggles and experiences that had shaped them. So it is difficult to know why they speak the way they do. Women had no difficulty in being open about the experiences that had shaped their lives. In the dialogue context, it was also instructive to know how much unstructured interfaith exposure they have had in the course of their day-to-day life and in their family relationships.

"In our round of introductions," reported Diana Eck to the working group, "many spoke of their own lives and experience with people of other faiths, making clear at the outset that the meeting of religious traditions does not take place far away or in a contrived context, but in the very grain and substance of our experience." Here is a sample of the interfaith experiences that had already impacted the Toronto group, from the notes taken by Diana Eck during the personal introductions:

> Lila Fahman from Saskachewan had launched the Council of Muslim Women in Canada, her father a shaykh, her mother a Methodist and her husband a Roman Catholic; both her mother and husband had become Muslims....
>
> There was Saroja Gupta, an Indo-Canadian Hindu whose son had become Catholic....
>
> Vasudha Narayanan, south Indian Vaishnava Hindu, had attended a Roman Catholic School and a Muslim college...
>
> There was Rabiatu Ammah from Ghana who said, "I have Muslims, Christians and African Traditionalists in my own family"...
>
> Judith Zimmer Brown, raised in Methodist household, became a Buddhist...
>
> Sylvia Boorstein, an American Buddhist and teacher of *vipasanna* meditation who was raised in a traditional Jewish family and had raised her children in that tradition...
>
> Lalitha Das from the women's centre in Bombay, where women of the Hindu, Muslim, Christian and Sikh communities work together on common women's issues...
>
> Akiko Yamashita from Japan who is the only Christian in the entire family, a fact that makes her dialogue with Buddhists an inextricable part of daily life...[4]

The list could be continued. Each woman had a story to tell. Many of them had already been in a dialogue of life with other traditions. Through this experience, some of them had been confirmed in their faith; others had picked up courage to cross over to another tradition to experience it from the inside; still others, like two from the Native American tradition, honestly admitted that they had not only never met a Sikh before, but also had never heard that such a religious community existed.

I found myself comparing this with introductions given at meetings where the majority are made up of men. Men say where they work and what they do. Women say who they are and what their experience has been, which immediately opens up a dialogue at quite a different level.

The last feature I noticed is something that I had anticipated. It had to do with the common experience of women as women across all religious communities.

The preparatory group of women had chosen six topics for conversation: scripture, Tradition, leadership, role model, authority and sexuality. We need not go into the details of the discussion of each of these topics. But, as anticipated, the subordination of women in the structures of organized religions, and the experience of women as the subordinated, with minor variations, were common to all the religious traditions without exception.

The women also pointed out that the founders of some of the religions, like Jesus, Buddha and the Prophet had attempted to bring about changes in the situation of women within their societies, but that in the subsequent evolution and interpretation of the scriptures and in the development of the traditions the advances thus made had been reversed. Most traditions pushed women back into a subordinate position, fixed their roles in the family and society, barred them from interpreting scriptures and denied them the kind of leadership that would bring about real change.

It is not my intention to go into the contents of the fascinating dialogue that the women had on these topics, weaving together the lived experience in the eight traditions that were represented in Toronto. A camera crew of women from "Vision TV", Canada, recorded these conversations and edited and presented them in six video tapes. These have since been televised nationwide in Canada, and have also been shown on several other occasions.[5]

My purpose in highlighting this event is to demonstrate that addressing the absence of women in dialogue goes much deeper than simply being open to having more women at dialogue meetings, although its importance should not be minimized.

The real problems lie in the heart of religious traditions themselves. The sexism that pervades religious traditions is also reflected in their dialogue with one another. And the dialogue enterprise, in so far as it accommodates this reality in the interest of promoting interfaith understanding, *is* compromised.

The reality of this compromise cannot be denied. But it is also important to recognize the dilemma that the ministry of dialogue faces in its attempt to promote interfaith relations and at the same time address the urgent issue of sexism in all religious traditions. For instance, in our attempt to bring together representatives of the Christian and Islamic communities in countries where the two communities live in a situation of conflict, it is important to bring together the leaders of these communities, people who can speak with some authority for their respective groups, and who would have some chance of implementing the recommendations of the meeting in their local situations. When we put together a list of persons with these "credentials", most of the time, it would turn out to be all men, simply because of the situation on the ground.

"We cannot go with this list," we would say in the staff planning meeting; "we need to make sure that women are well represented." Then the search would begin to identify women participants for the event, sometimes through insisting that our partners in the local scene, Christian as well as Muslim, name women who might be asked to participate. Finally the meeting would have some women, heavily outnumbered by men, and at times not listened to by the leadership of their own community at the meeting.

Fortunately the situation has been changing during the past few decades. In some of the religious traditions more and more women have been accepted as leaders and representatives. In all religious traditions there are well-qualified women with a sound knowledge of their traditions and their contemporary histories. Men in leadership positions are also becoming aware of the importance of involving women as representatives and spokespersons. These developments challenge those involved in the dialogue ministry to identify such women, to provide opportunity for them to participate, and to design the meetings in such a way that the voice of women and their related concerns become a normal part of the agenda. The dialogue ministry cannot afford to wait for radical changes within the religious traditions in order to have meaningful participation of women. Rather, dialogue events should continue to be catalysts for this to happen within all religious traditions.

Ursula King is rightly dissatisfied with the situation. "It is evident that inter-religious dialogue remains part of patriarchy," she says. "To envision and develop a post-patriarchal dialogue, it will be necessary to do away with all exclusions and hierarchies, especially the hierarchy of gender which is so pervasive in religion. Radical institutional and doctrinal transformations are needed to respond to the need of women for equal participation and dignity, and the demand to condemn all prejudice and violence against women, especially those done in the name of religion."[6]

In her account of the Toronto meeting, Eck deals with the same issue, pointing out that the situation calls for a sixfold "revolution" – revolution of language, history, interpretation, experience, leadership and ritual. On each of these issues much needs to be done within all the religious traditions to make possible the fuller participation of women.

In the meantime, are the major dialogue programmes and the main interfaith organizations compromised? Are they indeed working within the structures of patriarchy?

The answer, painfully, is "yes".

It is of course true that a compromised dialogue is better than no dialogue at all, and that, as in all other matters, some realism and pragmatism have a place also in dialogue. But there is little justification for the continuation of the compromise.

There are, among others, four main reasons why dialogue activity must undergo a radical change in this area.

1. The importance of dialogue at the grassroots level. In the initial stages of the promotion of interfaith dialogue there was some justification for the leaders of the communities, their clergy and formal representatives, to participate in dialogue events. This gave important "signals" to communities that had for centuries seen themselves as rival communities, sometimes at war with each other. There was also some understandable nervousness in the initial stages on how a particular religion is presented in the dialogue context. Religious traditions were keen to be represented in dialogue events by those considered by the community as "official" interpreters of the tradition concerned. Unfortunately most persons with these "credentials" within all our religious traditions were men. This in itself must change, and is changing.

In the meantime, however, there are new pressures. The dialogue scene itself has passed this stage of its development. We now live in a world that has changed radically in a matter of decades. Population movements, communications technology, growing understanding of one another's religious traditions, the practice of adopting other spiritualities and similar developments have changed the character of the dialogue we need. We also witness a growing change in the religious consciousness which is moving away from a purely intellectual, dogmatic understanding of religion to a more experiential and intuitive one.

If the Toronto experience is anything to go by, the approach to dialogue and the actual practices of dialogue among women are more life-oriented; they come out of actual experiences, and they are more clearly oriented to bringing about concrete changes in perception and practice at the very basic level of the lives of people. In fact, dialogue among women makes more immediate connection to and use of the "dialogue of life" that is already present in all pluralistic situations. Although men are in day-to-day relationships in society, when they meet they put on new hats that mark them out as religious persons. When women meet they begin to build on what is already going on. This is not to draw stereotypes of men and women attributing "intellect" and "a dogmatic bias" to the one, and an "experiential" and "intuitive" orientation to the other. In the interfaith field itself there are several women with exceptional intellectual capacity and with solid training in theology and dogma. And yet, generally speaking, there are discernible differences between women and men in their approach to and practice of dialogue.

All this is not meant to idealize women and the dialogue among them; it is only to emphasize that in today's world we need a dialogue that is life-oriented, one that will make a difference at the level of the lives of ordinary people. It is to underline the need for a dialogue that builds on our experience of living in a pluralistic world. Women's approach to dialogue and its practice is oriented to this reality.

2. *The importance of feeding the new thinking into the dialogue.* It is no secret that the awakening of women to their situation has gathered such momentum in recent decades that all religions, some more openly than others, some more willingly than others, are in the process of rethinking the place of women within religion and society. In any case, in all religions there are distinct and audible voices, of both women and men, which challenge some of the traditional language, imagery, teachings and structures. At one time these used to happen in the margins of religious life. But today they are increasingly part of the mainstream thinking. The signs of the changes are seen in our daily life.

Some years ago the writings of feminist scholars appeared in the "longer booklist" recommended for courses in theology. Today they are part of the required texts. Some years back, if a rabbi was to come and give an address at the seminary, one invariably expected a man to show up. Today a young woman rabbi may show up and give a penetrating analysis of what it means to be a Jew in a pluralistic society. At one time only men were interpreters of the Quran. Today there are feminist readings of the Quran, critical of the way tradition has distorted the intentions of the Quran and of the Prophet.

In any authentic dialogue these voices and issues can no longer be absent. A dialogue without these voices distorts the religious reality of our day.

3. The importance of dialogue for the new thinking that is emerging. All religious traditions today are in the process of revisiting their traditional teachings in response to the pressures of the contemporary realities. This is not a new phenomenon. Religious traditions have always adapted their core teachings in response to changes in society. One of the courses I remember vividly from my own seminary days was on "the history of Christian doctrine". It told the story of how doctrines developed in dialogue with society, culture and the philosophies of particular periods. It helped me to take doctrinal formulations seriously, but not too seriously.

The recognition of plurality and the practice of interfaith dialogue are among the factors that influence religious thinking in our day. Christian theology today cannot be done without an awareness of what other people believe. In fact the way other religious traditions have dealt with some of the deep mysteries of life can throw significant light on Christian thinking.

Given this reality, it is unfortunate, as King points out, that much of the feminist theology takes place outside the engagement in interfaith dialogue. Even as dialogue needs the thinking of women, women need the context of dialogue for a theology that would address more adequately the pluralistic world from the perspective of women. Women's theological work will be incomplete to the extent that it does not take religious pluralism with the seriousness it deserves. But this cannot happen unless women are fully represented in dialogues and sufficient opportunities are created for women themselves to compare notes across religious barriers.

We already have an example of such isolated development in the Latin American theology of liberation, which had for some time taken only socio-political reality as the context for doing theology. Asian and African theologians had to challenge Latin American theologians to take also the religio-cultural context seriously, so that their theology would not leave out part of the crucial data essential to any theological reflection.

The involvement of women and women's issues is important not only for the dialogue, but also for feminist thought. There is much room here for mutual correction and mutual enrichment.

4. The importance of signs and signals. I recall a discussion in the WCC when a pastoral team of four persons had to be put together to visit a difficult conflict situation. The group that worked on the composition came up with a list of five names which included confessional and regional balance. But all five were men. "We have tried to build all the balances including the gender balance," one of the colleagues explained, "but by the time we built in the confessional balance important for this occasion and the expertise needed we ran into a problem with gender balance."

The list of names was convincing, and one could easily see why each one on the list had to be on this team visit. When we were almost ready to approve the list through a conspiracy of silence, one of the colleagues asked the disturbing question: "What signal would we be giving to the churches by sending an all-male team?"

Finally the whole process had to be gone through once again in order to come up with a team of three men and two women. The question that prompted the reopening of the discussion has remained with me.

"What signal would we give?" if we could not find a single woman in our over 300 member churches in over a hundred countries of five hundred million people who could be on this team visit? That we could not find a woman who was pastoral enough to be part of a pastoral team going to a conflict situation? That it is in order for the churches, where more than half of the worshippers are women, to be represented by five men? That women would not be able to "connect" to the people in a conflict where the majority of the displaced are women and children? That it is in order for the churches to think only of men when they want to put a team together?

This is also important when we look at dialogue. What signals do we give?

Are religions a men's affair, and dialogue men's activity? Are women not able to enter into meaningful dialogue? Do we believe that women's perspectives do not make a difference to dialogue? And do we think that in all our dialogue men are able to speak for themselves and also for all women?

But this is precisely the signal that the dialogue work of all the major actors has given to most women. This may well be the reason why women who wish to rethink the faith are not looking to dialogue as an appropriate place for it, despite the wealth of thought in the world of religions and the benefits of doing theology for the wider community. This is the signal that leads King to conclude that "interfaith dialogue remains part of patriarchy".

To Christians in dialogue it is also now a question of witness – of the kind of community we believe in and aspire to be.

Where dialogue is compromised, our witness too will remain compromised.

NOTES

[1] Diana L. Eck, "Dialogue: A Vital Concern within the Ecumenical Movement", in *The Challenge of Dialogue: Papers from the Meeting of the Dialogue Working Group*, Casablanca, Morocco, 1989, Geneva, WCC, 1989, pp.21-22.
[2] Ursula King, "Feminism: The Missing Dimension in the Dialogue of Religions", in John D'Arcy May, ed., *Pluralism and the Religions: The Theological and Political Dimensions*, London, Cassell, 1998, pp.42-43.

72

[3] *Ibid.*, pp.40-55.
[4] *Op. cit.*, pp.23-24.
[5] A brief summary of the discussions under these topics, and the lessons to be drawn from them for dialogue are to be found in Diana Eck's moderator's report cited above.
[6] *Op. cit.*, p.52.

5. Socio-Political Issues and the Credibility of Dialogue

Of all the criticism levelled against dialogue, for me the most troubling is that which questions its credibility. It does not question one or another of the aspects, methods or results of dialogue, but the whole enterprise. To question the credibility of dialogue is to cast doubts on the goals and purpose of the exercise, of the sincerity and seriousness of those engaged in it. It is a way of saying: "No, we don't want to have anything to do with it!"

The questioning of the credibility of dialogue comes from several angles. Sometimes it is based on justifiable reasons. At other times it arises from wrong perceptions of what is being done, misunderstanding of the intentions or suspicions about its purpose and goals.

If dialogue is primarily about promoting mutual understanding and community, why should anyone call its credibility in question?

Doubts about the intention

The question of other faiths had occupied the WCC since its inception, and there had been a prolonged and broad-based study on the "Word of God and the Living Faiths of Men" [*sic*] through the 1950s and 1960s. This study had also led to the first serious discussions on the concept of "dialogue" at an important meeting in Kandy (1967) and at the WCC assembly in Uppsala (1968). These, however, were discussions among Christians themselves.

One of the landmarks in the WCC's dialogue journey was the first interfaith dialogue meeting, held in Ajaltoun, Lebanon, in March 1970, organized by Stanley Samartha, with the approval of the meeting of the WCC central committee in August 1969. It was an interfaith dialogue on "dialogue". It brought together three Hindus, four Buddhists, three Muslims and several Christians to explore the meaning and significance of "dialogue" as a new basis for relationships among religious traditions.

A fourth Hindu invited to the meeting turned down the invitation, and in a letter he questioned the whole *intention* of Christians in turning to "dialogue" as a way of relating to neighbours of other faiths. In his view, Christians never give up their intention to convert Hindus and others to their own faith. Since most of the other missionary methods have failed, they now turn to dialogue as a new strategy of mission.[1]

Although such straightforward statements are rarely made at dialogue meetings, the suspicion about the true intentions of dialogue on the part of Christians has plagued the dialogue venture from the beginning. Christians themselves contribute to this suspicion. The "mission-dialogue" debates at some major WCC conferences and assemblies have taken place in the presence of guests of other faiths. There, several Christians who opposed dialogue have insisted that the great commission demands that we bring the whole world to Christ, through whom alone salvation is mediated to the world. Therefore the only legitimate dialogue is the one through which Christ is proclaimed as the saviour.

People of other traditions understand the particularity of faiths and the legitimacy of witnessing to one's convictions. But the excessive obsession with "converting the whole world to Christ" makes them nervous. This is further aggravated by some sections in the more conservative groups within the church, who support dialogue without any hesitation, but only as a tool of mission. "We should respect the other faiths and have a full knowledge of their beliefs, enter into a closer relationship with them and refrain from judgmental attitudes," they would say, "so that we might proclaim the gospel at the appropriate moment, and lead them to Christ."

Neighbours of other faiths, therefore, receive mixed signals. While groups of Christians appear to be advocating an open, genuinely mutual and trusting relationship committed to the creation of a community of communities that would live in peace with each other and in mutual witness, other groups are bent on converting them to Christ.

Another dimension of this ambiguous signal is the kind of position that the late Lesslie Newbigin held, in which there is affirmation both of dialogue and a traditional understanding of mission. Newbigin insisted that both are possible and needed, and that they must be separated. There are times, he said, when he was in a "dialogue" with his Hindu neighbour, and there are times when he was in "mission", proclaiming Christ as the one way of salvation that God has offered to all humankind.

It would appear that each time a Hindu meets with a Christian, he or she must ask, "Which mood are you in?" before deciding whether to continue the conversation!

Over the years, the actual practice of dialogue has convinced the partners in dialogue of the good faith of Christians involved in it. From the beginning those promoting dialogues have also made clear that all dialogue partners come with firm convictions which need not be suspended, hidden or denied. There has also been clarity about the place of mutual witnesses in dialogue, and of mutual correction, enrichment, transformation and even of the "risk" of crossing over when one engages in depth about other ways of being and believing.

I believe that through the patient, sustained and responsible work done during the stormy initial years by the Dialogue sub-unit, under the leadership of Samartha, dialogue has received credibility both within the church and among other religious traditions. Now interfaith dialogue is advocated by sections within all religions, governments and international organizations.

And yet the Christian schizophrenia on this matter is evident from time to time, when we hear bold, empty and triumphalistic pronouncements about the "Christianization of Europe", "bringing the world to Christ by the year 2000", "India for Christ" and so on. Such rhetoric may be necessary to ease the Christian conscience in a context marked by an alarming lack of credible, sustained and demanding witness to the gospel in life and society. But they send signals of Christian intransigence and of a "hidden agenda" behind all Christian activities that seeks to conquer the world to Christianity.

76

Christian credibility in the area of dialogue can only be fully established when we have a theology, a theology of mission, and a theology of religions that address the continuing ambiguity, and come to terms with the reality of a religiously plural world which, in the words of Wilfred Cantwell Smith, "is the only world there is".

Doubts about our commitments

The WCC world mission conference in San Antonio (May 1989) had for its theme "Your Will be Done: Mission in Christ's Way". Section II of the conference worked on the subject of "participating in suffering and struggle". In preparation for the discussions in this section, teams of participants had been sent to selected areas in the world where communities were suffering and were involved in struggles for peace with justice. Among the areas the organizers had selected were the West Bank refugee camps.

During the conference those who went on the team visits were to report to the section, and the section, based on the discussion, was to prepare a report to the plenary.

The Israeli-Palestinian issue has of course been a long-standing concern within the WCC, and the WCC has made many statements on the situation. The WCC is in dialogue with both Jews and Muslims and has member churches in all parts of the Middle East. It has also been active in the discussions on the future of Jerusalem. Following the second world war and the *Shoah* (holocaust), the WCC had taken a very strong stand against antisemitism and had supported the cause of the Jewish people. Following the Israeli occupation of Arab and Palestinian territories, the WCC took an equally strong stand calling for the Israeli withdrawal from the occupied territories. Within the member churches of the WCC there are powerful voices, especially from Europe and North America, that speak up for the Jewish cause, linking the welfare and security of the state of Israel with the welfare of the Jewish people. There are other equally strong voices calling the WCC to condemn Israel and to give unreserved support to the Palestinians. There are those who advocate that we must completely separate the state of Israel from our solidarity with the Jewish people, and others who see the future of Jewish people linked to a secure Jewish state, arguing that without a strong state Jews would be thrown back to their vulnerable pre-war situation as a weak and scattered community.

Although statements on such situations are prepared for the WCC by its Commission on International Affairs, which has followed the developments carefully through the years and carefully weighs each word used in the statements, after every statement issued the Dialogue Sub-unit would receive telephone calls, sometimes from our Jewish partners, critical that the WCC is not sensitive to the real threats faced by the Jewish community, and at other times from the Islamic and Christian communities, accusing the WCC of dragging its feet and not speaking out for the Palestinians. Often the statements made leave both parties dissatisfied.

What would a section on "suffering and struggle" at a mission conference, which had only heard a report from a group of persons who had visited Palestinian refugee camps, say in its statement? It was not too difficult to guess. But there were participants at the conference from churches which have always been sensitive to Jewish concerns. To complicate matters, the conference, for the first time in the history of mission conferences, had invited persons of other faiths, including representatives of Jewish and Islamic communities, as guests. Here indeed were all the ingredients for a heated, inconclusive and deeply divisive confrontation.

The situation was saved only because the conference ran out of time to have any meaningful discussion on any of the four section reports!

Anticipating an inconclusive controversy, I had approached the section leadership to share the section report with the dialogue staff before it was finalized. "If you just share it with those dealing with Christian-Jewish and Christian-Muslim relations they may pick up anything that is likely to be too offensive," I said.

But I learned later that some in the leadership of the drafting group decided that this was not a good idea. "The Christian-Jewish dialogue", in the opinion of the spokesperson, "was overly committed to the Jewish cause. It will support only those positions that are agreeable to the Jews. And the Jews in the dialogue are only interested in the subjects of 'antisemitism' and the 'protection of the state of Israel'. One cannot expect solidarity with the Palestinians."

It was obvious that the person concerned was not fully aware of the complexities involved in maintaining dialogue with all parties in situations of conflict. Further, Jews and Christians, within the WCC's dialogue programme, have been meeting in recent years in South Africa, South Asia and North Asia and other places to dialogue on a broad range of subjects such as "Tradition", "heritage" and "wisdom". There is great diversity of opinion within the Jewish community itself on the Palestinian issue and an increasing plurality of Jewish dialogue partners in conversation with the WCC. Solidarity with the sufferings of the Palestinians was not in danger in a conversation with the "dialogue people". If anything, such a conversation would have strengthened the intention of the document to support the just causes of the Palestinians by removing any anti-Jewish rhetoric which would distract discussion of the central concerns of the statement at the plenary. There was no need to play "hide-and-seek"!

Nor do complaints about credibility relate to any one particular interfaith relationship. Similar complaints have been made about WCC's Muslim-Christian relations by some Christians in Pakistan and Nigeria, for example, accusing the programme of "soft-pedaling" in order not to offend Muslims.

Dialogue would of course lose all credibility if it remained at the level of relationship for its own sake. At the same time there is little awareness that dialogue cannot happen if the relationships are broken off in the first instance. It is possible to take up tough issues within the dialogue context. But we need patience and prudence; the ability to speak as well as the willingness to listen.

Dialogue is built on trust; it thrives on openness.

Doubts about our partners

"The whole dialogue programme of the WCC in relation to India has no credibility at all," a bishop once told me in Madras, "because your partners are our oppressors." The statement was rather strong and categorical; it reflected anger and disapproval. For me, it was a debatable statement on an issue that required deeper analysis. But that was not the time to argue, but to listen.

The issue the bishop raised is a real problem in relation to our dialogue with Hindu partners, especially in India. It relates to the rigid caste structure and the pervasive caste consciousness in India, where some 20 percent of the population, about 200 million people, are considered "outcastes" or "untouchables". Since caste and untouchability are acquired through birth, and the possibility for upward mobility is limited, the "outcastes" have been an oppressed group in India through the centuries. Even though untouchability has been abolished in the law, the practice continues in rural India (where 80 percent of the population lives) and persists in the social consciousness of people throughout the country. The rigidity of the social structure that maintains it and the level of oppression and indignity that they suffer have led some to call the phenomenon of untouchability the "apartheid of India".

There are quite a few inconclusive debates about the origins of the caste system and of untouchability. The basic ordering of society into a social hierarchy, especially into the four major castes *(varnas)* of *Brahmana* (priests, intellectuals), *Ksatriya* (warriors, administrators), *Vaisyas* (farmers, traders) and *Sudra* (labourers) is supported in the *Rig Veda*, the most sacred of the holy texts of Hinduism. In the course of history these four major castes divided further into numerous sub-castes or *jatis*, with their own hierarchy. The most disturbing aspect of the development is the leaving out of a group as the "outcastes", who were not only required to do the most menial of jobs in society but were also considered ritually impure and not even to be touched and, according to some interpretations, not even to be seen.

Today the community considered untouchable calls itself *dalit*, meaning the oppressed, the broken or the crushed. Many dalits consider themselves to be the original inhabitants of India who were overcome by the Aryan invaders (though this theory is contested by others). They do not consider Hinduism, with its caste manifestations, as their religion but as one that suppressed the original traditional religion of India to which they belonged, and is still manifested in dalit culture.

The missionary movement of the 18th and 19th centuries had its greatest success among the dalit communities, with the result that 75-80 percent of Christians in India are of dalit origin.

The *Brahmanas*, commonly called "Brahmins", the caste of intellectuals and priests, were the main exponents of Hindu philosophies and the ones who performed the rituals and interpreted the teachings. They were the custodians of the *varna dharma* or the caste system. They, more than others, consider even the sight of an untouchable as ritually polluting. As the caste that had the privilege through the centuries to be the interpreters of Hinduism, Brahmins even today dominate the Hindu religious scene, especially as its intellectual exponents.

We need not go into a complex discussion of the origin and practice of the caste system; our purpose is only to give some background for the bishop's comment, "your partners are our oppressors". In his view, classical Hinduism, in so far as it commends a caste-based society, and the mainstream Hindus, in so far as they practise the caste system, are not appropriate partners for dialogue. To be in dialogue with them would be to compromise; it would amount to a tacit approval of the caste system by the Christian partners. More importantly it amounts to a lack of concern for and solidarity with the oppressed community. The bishop is not alone in expressing such disapproval. Many who are involved in the social struggle for the liberation of the dalits see relationship and dialogue with "Brahminical" or "classical" Hinduism as an exercise that questions the credibility of dialogue which aims at building community.

I was at first inclined to agree with the bishop and all who hold his view. As someone who has lived for nearly a decade in India, and travelled widely in the villages, I am well aware of the gross injustices done to dalits and of the indignities they suffer from day to day. Liberation of the dalits is a cause that should be espoused by anyone concerned with justice in human relationships. I am also aware that the caste system is rooted in "mainline" Hinduism, and that scriptures and religious literature are often used to defend it.

Should we, then, suspend our dialogue with Hindus in mainstream Hinduism because the social structure is oppressive? Does dialogue with classical Hinduism amount to a betrayal of the dalit cause? Will dialogue lose its credibility by having relationships with Hindus of the "higher" castes? I have agonized over these questions partly because, at that time, it was my responsibility within the WCC to develop relationships with Hindus and Buddhists.

While in solidarity with the dalit cause, I do not however agree with the bishop for several reasons. First, nearly 60 percent of the Indian population belong to what may be called "caste Hinduism", that is, to one or another of the existing castes. To say that we should not converse with "higher" Hinduism is to cut off our contacts with the religion of a substantial part of the Indian population.

Second, all religious communities, at different times in history or within one or another streams of interpretation of their faith, have had manifestations that provoked hostile reactions from others. While there may be occasions when we must dissociate ourselves from attitudes and practices that lead to large-scale discrimination, we cannot insist in the first instance that a community's teachings, ethical and moral conduct or structures should be acceptable to us in order to enter into dialogue.

Third, I feel that the bishop had not given sufficient allowance for the internal plurality and diversity within what he calls Hinduism. Hinduism indeed has great internal diversity. It has produced among its own religious leaders, including the Brahmins, many spiritual leaders who have fought caste and untouchability. There have also been several movements within Hinduism that have sought to break down the caste barriers.

Fourth, while caste and untouchability are unacceptable features of the social structure, Hinduism has also been the cradle of some of the highest and deepest philosophical thoughts, of some of the most moving devotional poetry and refined forms of art, architecture, music and drama. The argument that all these must be rejected because they emanate from an oppressive religion is not convincing. And we cannot forget that such ambiguity besets all religious traditions and their cultural heritage.

Lastly, the objections that are raised come out of a particular perception of what happens in a dialogue situation. I recall the first Hindu-Christian dialogue I organized under WCC auspices. Some fifteen Hindus and fifteen Christians were brought together at Rajpur in the foothills of the Himalayas. The Hindu side had a good mix; among them were Brahmin professors, swamis and social activists from across the caste barriers. The Christian side also had a mix, including Christians drawn from "dalit" and "caste" backgrounds. The topic was "Religious Resources for a Just Society".

Debated at the meeting were questions of caste and untouchability, problems of the authority and interpretation of scriptures, and conditions for justice in society. There were lively disagreements among Christians and among Hindus as much as between Christians and Hindus. There were deep disagreements among the caste Hindus on the interpretation and application of scripture, as among Christians. The dialogue gave an opportunity for caste Hindus to listen to the dalit perspective and for dalits to recognize the struggle of some people within caste Hinduism to come to terms with concerns of justice. In the Indian context, Christians are left with little choice but to engage the phenomenal reality of traditional Hinduism. Yet a dialogue with Hindus which ignores or sacrifices the cause of the dalits would be a betrayal of the gospel. Here dialogue and witness need to go hand in hand.

The credibility, then, has to do not so much with who our partners are, but with what we are prepared to talk about and what we hope to achieve through the process.

It is interesting to note the ambivalence of Christians on this question. For a long time there were complaints about our partners in Christian-Muslim relations. "You are talking to the Westernized, liberal Muslims on subjects that are of little consequence to the churches" – that was a common criticism. The Christian-Muslim programme began to respond to this concern by developing relations with Islamic world organizations and with accepted Muslim leadership in Sudan, Nigeria, Egypt, Iran and other countries. By the time a third delegation of Muslims visited the WCC there was some concern. "What is the WCC doing with the Muslims of Iran?" a colleague asked, showing some nervousness.

Dialogue. What else?

I do not mean to defend all the activities that go on in the name of dialogue. Dialogue can be genuine, committed, engaging, difficult, and aimed at building community. But it can also be used as a tool to manipulate others or to promote one's own concerns. It can remain unproductive, promoting shallow amiability, or play into the hands of idealists who think that they have found the solution to unite all humankind. It can be used as a platform by those who want public recognition or social legitimacy. Dialogue can be abused as a front to cover up deep injustices in a community and used as a public relations stunt to gain respectability. It can be thought of as a method to gain leadership, and control of the religious scene.

During my twelve years in the WCC sub-unit on Dialogue, I have seen something of all these. It was part of my mandate to try to discern which aims at what, and to relate to each of them.

In my speeches and writings I have often used the phrases "the dialogue ministry" or "the ministry of dialogue". As far as I am aware, I was the first person who, however unconsciously, brought the words "ministry" and "dialogue" together. It may simply be part of my Methodist heritage, but I think there is more to it.

The English word "ministry" means "service". It points to what we do to facilitate the lives of others. Dialogue is a "service" aimed at facilitating life in community; it is a ministry. Already in Chiang Mai the *Guidelines on Dialogue* captured this spirit through describing it as "a fundamental part of Christian service within community" and a "joyful affirmation of life against chaos, and a participation with all who are the allies of life in seeking the provisional goals of a better human community".[2]

The credibility of dialogue, in the last analysis, will depend not so much on "with whom?" or "on what?", but "why?"

NOTES

[1] For the full report see S.J. Samartha, ed., *Dialogue between Men of Living Faiths*, Geneva, WCC, 1971.

[2] *Op. cit.*, pp.10-11.

6. Inter-religious Marriage: Problem or Promise?

When I was the minister of the Methodist church in Colombo, a young man from my congregation showed up at my home at Boswell Place one day.

"*Pothagar*," he said, and hesitated. I like the way a minister is addressed in Tamil. "*Pothagar*" simply means "teacher".

I asked him to take a seat. "I am planning to get married," the young man announced. "My mother asked me to see you." I was all smiles! I congratulated him and asked him when he was planning to have the wedding.

"But there is a problem," he said. "The girl is a Hindu."

In Sri Lanka a girl remains a "girl" until she is married. The designation "woman" is normally reserved for the married and for those who remained single beyond the normal age of marriage. Even at the university level, girls were "girls". When I first went to teach a course in the United States, I had to keep reminding myself that I did not have "girls" in my class, but "women students"!

"So, why did you decide to marry a Hindu girl?" I asked. That was a stupid question: I knew the answer.

"We fell in love; we had worked in the same place."

"Did you already know that she was a Hindu when you proposed to her?"

"Yes, but we understand each other very well; we don't anticipate any problem because of religious difference."

"Of course not!" – this time I was talking to myself. When two persons are in love, they have limitless confidence in what they can achieve together. They do not believe and certainly do not want to be told that perhaps they should anticipate some problems, and that they need to think more deeply about them before making their vows to each other.

The young man had come to find out if I could marry them in church, if her parents agreed. The woman's parents and the woman herself were not keen that she should become a Christian just for the sake of marriage, which was quite understandable.

At the same time, the rules of the church forbade marriage in the church unless both the man and the woman were

Christians. They also forbade a service of blessing of the marriage in the church, or even at a home, if the Christian partner was marrying according to another religious rite.

There was little I could do in terms of the ceremony, except to offer a service of blessing, and that only if they had a civil marriage ceremony. While assuring my personal support to the couple and my willingness to meet them and help them in other ways, I told him that as far as the ceremony was concerned, the rules are laid down by the Methodist conference and I had little choice in what I might do.

The young man looked disappointed. Perhaps he thought that on these matters I could make all the decisions! He was also facing for the first time (apart from the initial resistance to the idea from the parents on both sides) the inbuilt resistance in all religious traditions to marriage outside their own faith.

I was also aware, having ministered to other couples in interfaith marriages, that the problem they were facing about the kind of marriage ceremony they would have was only the beginning of the series of difficult issues they would have to face together in the years ahead – of the religion of the home, the public practice of their respective religions, the religious affiliation of their children, religious education of the children, festivals to be celebrated, rites to be observed and so on.

Only months earlier a colleague had told me how sometimes the problems persisted even after one's death. A Hindu had married a Christian woman of his congregation. Even though the man never accepted baptism or officially became a Christian himself, he allowed his children to be baptized and had regularly attended the church with the family. When the man died, the wife wanted to give him a Christian burial. But his brothers and sisters insisted that he should be cremated according to the Hindu rite because he had never converted to Christianity or accepted baptism as a mark of it. They could not come to an agreement, and my colleague had to come up with the compromise that the body be first cremated, then he would preside over an act of burial of the ashes!

A neglected topic

My encounter with the young man is by no means an isolated event. In pluralistic societies, where people are thrown together in their day-to-day life, it is only natural that women and men meet across racial, ethnic and religious barriers and at times enter into a deeper relationship of love and commitment. This is only to be expected. Studies have shown that interfaith marriages are on the increase, especially in the Western hemisphere.

Some years ago I was involved with the Ecumenical Institute for Study and Dialogue in Colombo in facilitating a meeting of mixed marriage couples. The intention was to learn how far religious communities had been assisting these couples before and after the marriage, and to learn how the couples themselves were coping with the challenge of bringing the experience of two different religious traditions under one roof.

The first thing we learned was that none of the religious traditions had any meaningful way of addressing the issue. None had any plan to prepare the couple before marriage or accompany them pastorally after marriage. In Buddhism and Hinduism there was no concept of an organized pastoral accompaniment. In Christianity, where the concept is an important component of the ministry, the help they got depended entirely on the minister/priest concerned. In the case of the couples who had gathered together, none could speak of any sustained help from the church or the church community.

There were three reasons that were mentioned to explain the effective isolation of the couple. The first is that, especially within the Christian and the Islamic traditions, when a person decides to marry a Buddhist or a Hindu there is a sense of "betrayal" among members of the community concerned. It is considered a "less than Christian" or "less than Islamic" thing to do. It is taken as a signal given by the person concerned of readiness to "leave" the community, even though that is never intended. In any case these communities, as religious communities, have not developed any mechanism to welcome and be hospitable to a person of another religion within their community. Therefore a person who married outside the community is considered as one who has "left" them.

The second reason seems to lie in the behaviour of the couple. Having faced initial antagonism from parents and relatives, and a refusal to be accommodating on the part of their religious community, the couple lose all confidence in looking to these sources for support, even when the marriage runs into trouble. In almost all cases of interfaith marriages (except those in which one partner had "converted" to the religion of the other) the couples felt that they have to "fix" their own problems. In much of Asia and Africa, where there is little or no professional marriage counselling, couples with marital problems would turn (often as a last resort) to a trusted relative or the religious leader for counselling and support. But this one outlet is closed when a person is perceived to have "left" his or her respective community.

The Christian clergy present at the conference gave the third reason. Often they are reluctant to maintain contact with the Christian partner in an interfaith marriage (after the marriage) for fear of being accused of interference. Often such contacts are misunderstood as attempts to keep the Christian partner in his or her faith and to "grab" the children to the faith, or as a subtle attempt to convert the partner of the other faith into the Christian fold. Unfortunately some Christian clergy do act in this manner, bringing disruption into the family. Others keep out for fear of being accused of such a motive.

Thus the couple are left to fend for themselves. Some of them continue to have a sense of guilt, and all of them have the tendency to attribute to religious incompatibility even the most natural problems of relationship that arise in any marriage.

The second fact that struck us at the meeting of mixed marriage couples is that no two such marriages are identical. No two couples have handled in the same way the adjustments needed to bring two religious traditions into one family. It would appear that ways of handling the interfaith situation in mixed marriages are as many as there are such marriages. This is mainly because there is no "standard" or typical Christian, Hindu, Buddhist or Muslim. Their knowledge, commitment, practice and attachment to the respective religious traditions, and their knowledge of and attitude and affinity to the religious tradition of their spouses are so different that no two couples have had the same experience of the level of tolerance and accommodation within an interfaith marriage.

The easiest situation was where one of the spouses, for whatever reason, formally converted to the faith of the other and was willing to respect that decision for the rest of their married life. Next was the situation where one of the partners was deeply committed to the faith while the other was only nominally religious and had no desire to prescribe the faith for the children. Here the religion of the practising partner became the religion of the home and of the children, with a casual or an increasingly committed involvement of the other.

In most cases interfaith marriages survived through religion taking a back seat in the lives of the partners, by their having little or nothing to do with the religious communities they had come from, and by not discussing "religion" at home. But this "undeclared peace" is often disrupted with the arrival of children. Even those who do not practise their religion suddenly become deeply conscious of their religious identity when the children come. They would like the children to go through what they had gone through as children. In some religious traditions the eldest child, especially the son, is expected to perform special religious rites at the death of the parents. This becomes a major issue for some of the spouses.

Many testify that the hope that "all will be well because we love each other" begins to run into trouble with the arrival of children. This is the time when most couples come to the point of needing to talk things over. Sometimes it can be a creative conversation leading to a mutually acceptable arrangement. At other times it leads to fierce arguments, quarrels and even break-ups. This is also the time when couples realize how inadequate their preparation for the marriage has been. Often there is a sense of being betrayed by the partner, the feeling that he or she is going back on understandings that had been assumed to exist, and that there is insensitivity to the feelings and needs of the other.

The arrangements made for the children are also ad hoc and differ from family to family. They range from dividing the children between the faiths to the decision not to bring them up in any faith. The idealistic approach is to expose children to both religions in the hope that they, when "old enough", will choose from among the two faiths, or to bring them up "multifaith"!

In all these problems related to the children too, the religious communities offered no help to the couples except, of course, their readiness to accept the children into their fold any time.

Not all the stories were so negative. Quite a few of those who marry across faith traditions have enough resourcefulness, trust and love to resolve the problems that crop up, and have a happy married life. There are couples who show a healthy respect for each other's faith and support each other in the practice of it. Some couples also manage to relate to each other's religious communities. Some make advance decisions on how they will bring up their children, so that the arrival of the child does not precipitate a crisis for the family. There are rare occasions where the couple enter into a deeper dialogue about their respective religious traditions, thus learning more about each other's faith backgrounds.

The overall impression, however, is one of being abandoned by the religious communities to which they had belonged. The success of an interfaith marriage depended entirely on the couples themselves.

In 1994 the Office of Inter-religious Relations of the WCC and the Vatican's Pontifical Council for Inter-religious

Dialogue launched a joint enquiry into this subject, mainly in response to increasing numbers of inter-religious marriages in Europe, especially among Christians and Muslims. In the absence of any organized help from the religious bodies themselves, many of the local churches and congregations were developing "pastoral guidelines" and "resources" to help these couples. The purpose of the joint study was to make a survey of the situation and the resource material available, to document the experience of people in inter-religious marriages and to lift up the concerns that should receive greater attention in the future.

In terms of the experience of the couples and the attitude of and assistance from the religious communities, the study confirmed many of the findings of the Colombo meeting. There was one important innovation in the materials produced in Europe. In addition to general information, they also attempted to inform those contemplating interfaith marriages of the legal implications of marriages across traditions, especially if they also involve the crossing of national boundaries. For example, if an Algerian Muslim living in France were to marry a Reformed Christian woman from France, under what laws would the marriage be conducted? What would be the conjugal rights of the man and of the woman? How do the religious laws of Islam and of the Reformed Church apply to such marriages? What are the rules governing divorce, if the marriage were to fail? Who would have the custody of children? What are the laws of inheritance? If they decided to go to Algeria and live there, what would be the status of the marriage? If the Algerian were to become a French citizen what impact would it have on the laws governing their marriage?

When an Algerian man and a French woman fall in love and decide to enter into a marriage relationship these questions do not often occur to them. Later in their marriage, especially if the marriage runs into trouble, all these questions become important, and one or the other is completely surprised over what they had legally entered into through their contract of marriage.

The findings of the joint study, which aimed primarily at identifying the areas of concern, have been published.[1]

The cultural aspect of inter-religious marriages is another area where some assistance is called for. A European woman marrying a Hindu man sometimes has no idea of the continued importance of the family and community for someone from Asia, and of the expectation that he will continue to support his parents and immediate relatives in many ways. The "I-married-you, not-your-family" argument would not meet a favourable response. In a similar manner, there are vast differences among cultures in their attitude to the extended family, to sexual behaviour, to the place of women, men and children in the family, to the way to bring up children and on such issues as the best use of money and time!

An inter-religious marriage that is also intercultural is programmed to fail unless the partners have been throughly secularized. Those who survive do so because of their openness and resourcefulness, or because one of them becomes resigned to suffer in silence or to cut himself or herself off from the religion or culture that had been so formative before the marriage.

And yet these marriages have traditionally received very little attention from the religious communities.

The need for new thinking

I do not mean to advocate inter-religious or intercultural marriages or to idealize them as perfect opportunities for inter-religious dialogue at depth. If our studies are anything to go by, such marriages are beset with more problems than possibilities. Rarely have couples managed to make them occasions for dialogue and mutual enrichment or to engage in a joint spiritual pilgrimage. In most cases there have been more arguments than dialogues. This is of course understandable; after all, inter-religious marriages take place because one is attracted to a person and not necessarily to the religion to which he or she belongs.

The concern, therefore, is not how to promote inter-religious marriages, but with how best to deal with them.

1. The new reality

A careful study of the attitude of religious communities shows that much of the way inter-religious marriages are handled still reflects the times when religious communities treated one another as mutually exclusive or rival groups. Therefore, the primary focus of regulations governing inter-religious marriages is punitive. They are designed to discourage and prevent such marriages, or when they do happen, to use them as opportunities for "conversion".

That kind of approach, whatever its merits or demerits, might have been tolerable when such marriages were few and far between. All the indications show that they are steadily on the increase, and the likelihood is that they may become even more common in future. This should come as no surprise, as more and more young people from different traditions study together in schools and universities and engage in leisure activities that throw them together. The social isolation of religious communities, the context of most marriages in the past, has completely broken down.

In addition, as mentioned earlier, not only have religious communities begun to live in close proximity, they have also begun to know each other. Religious leaders themselves give new signals through their engagements in interfaith events and activities. As a result, there is a new religious consciousness that enables people to accept people of other faiths and establish friendly relations with them. The words of Wilfred Cantwell Smith are relevant here as well. "However incipiently," says Smith, "the boundaries segregating off religious communities radically and finally from each other are beginning, just a little, to weaken or to dissolve, so that being a Hindu and being a Buddhist, or being a Christian and not being a Christian, are not so starkly alternatives as once seemed."[2]

Whether this is a good or a bad development is not the issue here. All religious communities recognize that there is a new inter-religious reality that is irreversible. They also, however grudgingly, welcome it. But the attitudes to inter-religious marriages and the rules that govern them show little recognition of this new reality. The time has come for the churches to review their policy on interfaith marriages in the light of their own new thinking on interfaith relations. But is it indeed possible for churches to review their policy without compromising their basic beliefs about marriage?

There is more room for flexibility here than is often assumed. At one time "mixed marriages" in Europe meant Protestant-Roman Catholic or Orthodox-Roman Catholic marriages. The same kinds of severe restriction were in place as regards these marriages as well, causing much suffering to those who married across confessional barriers. In a Protestant-Roman Catholic marriage, for example, the Roman Catholic Church held for a long time that its understanding of marriage and its ecclesiology made it difficult to accept these marriages, and especially to accept the family as a unit when members came to the eucharist. Thus while the couple might attend worship in both confessions they must receive the eucharist in different churches. Several conditions, including that of bringing up children in the Roman Catholic faith, were imposed in order for the validity of the marriage to be recognized.

The growing ecumenical consciousness, however, necessitated a change that makes it possible (at least in most places) to come to pastoral agreements that bring more room and greater relief to the families concerned.

A similar situation prevailed on the question of divorce in a number of churches. At one time marriage was understood as indissoluble under any circumstance. Gradually a number of church traditions, while still upholding the value of deep and lasting commitments, had to weigh the merits and demerits of forcing couples whose marriages had totally broken down to stick together, or to require a woman to continue to live with a man who was violent and abusive. In all societies, and in the Old and New Testaments, laws and regulations on marriage relationships take full account of concrete situations, also providing possibilities for separation where necessary.[3]

We are today in a new situation. Inter-religious marriages are likely to be on the increase, not because persons are less committed to their faith traditions, but because there is a new human reality in which old barriers are breaking down. All religious traditions should revisit their attitude and approach to persons who have found each other across the fences.

2. The pastoral dimension

What can be quite shocking to anyone who studies this issue is the sense of isolation, even of abandonment, felt by those who enter inter-religious marriages. Precisely at the time when the couple need guidance, support and help, the religious communities to which they had belonged (in some cases continually for more than twenty years) turn their back on them, refusing to offer a ceremony and gradually withdrawing from the couple for fear of being accused of interference.

The implications of this to our very understanding of "pastoral" ministry are so serious that many denominations have already begun to rethink the issue. Several churches now offer a wedding ceremony in the church if the other partner also desires it and is open to some orientation as regards the ceremony and its meaning. There is greater willingness to allow the Christian to be involved in ceremonies conducted by the religion of the other partner. Rules on "services of blessing" have been relaxed, and in some churches specially prepared liturgies for mixed marriages and services of blessings are included in the prayer book.

In some places there is also openness to extend invitations to the clergy of other religions to participate in the marriage ceremony. A Jewish rabbi and I shared in conducting a Jewish-Christian marriage service that had Christian and Jewish components. There is also an increased consciousness of the need for pastoral accompaniment and the practice of pre- and post-marital counselling. Much of this, however, still happens only when the marriage comes under the "wings" of the church and where the partner is willing to be ministered to by the church.

The pastoral issue, therefore, cannot be satisfactorily resolved unless there is greater contact between the two religious communities to which the couple belong so that they together will be able to provide a climate for such assistance. This will also enable the couple to relate to both communities and to be at home in both.

3. The theological dimension

Many of the formal arguments against inter-religious marriages are quasi-theological and call for a more thorough theological re-evaluation than can be attempted here.

Even though marriages are intended to be life-long, in many societies they are seen primarily as contractual, between two individuals or between their families or clans. This is the case even when they are formalized through elaborate religious rites and ceremonies in full public view. The contractual nature of the marriage is emphasized so that if one or the other does not live up to the commitments of the contract, necessary action can be taken to enforce the contract or to end it. This is based on the belief that marriages are primarily intended for human fulfilment.

Christianity, however, has moved in the direction of attributing more and more theological significance to marriage, to the point of almost eliminating the contractual dimension except as a moral and theological imperative. Thus, until laws have been relaxed in many churches in recent years, once married, the persons are caught in a trap with no escape door. Since the ultimate legitimacy of marriage is attributed more to the ceremony than to the contractual commitments, there was no provision to terminate it even when one or the other party completely violated the norms of relationship. Such theological mystification of marriage reaches its climax when it is held up as a "sacrament". If one were to study in depth the theology of marriage and its actual practice in the churches, one might well discover that the church has not done itself any great service by making a mystique of the relationship.

All societies recognize that a long, lasting and permanent relationship in marriage is ideal for the individuals involved, and especially for the children. This we must affirm. But most societies do not see "theological compulsion" as the best way to achieve it. Each society has designed practical ways to support marriages and to assist them as necessary. They have, however, refrained from attributing such high theological significance to the act of marriage or to the relationship within it. Much of the objection in the churches to inter-religious marriages is based on these theological reasons, which need to be re-examined.

A more convincing objection to inter-religious marriages has to do with the question of community. No person is an island; every person belongs to a community with its own symbol system for its own life in community and especially for expressing its relationship to God. It is argued that two persons who do not share a common symbol system will find it difficult to live together, and that persons who do not subscribe to the symbol system of a group cannot be welcomed into the community. Thus, one hears such statements as: "How can we hold a marriage ceremony between a Christian and a Hindu when we know that the Hindu does not have the same understanding of God as we do?"; "We cannot be part of a Buddhist ceremony because Buddhists do not have an explicit belief in God." This is a difficult question to resolve because it has to do with our theology of religions, our understanding of the relativity of religious language and symbol systems and the like. But even here much of the difficulty has to do with the traditional attitude of looking at religions as mutually exclusive. There is much more in common between religions than what separates them. In the past we made a virtue of emphasizing what is distinctive and different from others, primarily because our attitude to others was a mainly missionary one.

I remember being taken to a Buddhist temple in Japan just before an important ceremony was to take place. My hosts introduced me to the priest and told him that I was at an interfaith meeting organized by the WCC. Having received me with much grace, the priest told me something along these lines through the interpreter: "I am sorry that you may not fully understand what will be going on here, but you are most welcome to join us in this celebration."

Of course I did not understand what was taking place; it was in Japanese, and I was not too familiar with the Japanese expression of Buddhist faith. But I was very much there and was a part of it. My presence in no way interfered with their worship. Nor did it adversely affect my Christian faith. There was something more than "understanding" at work here. I was pleased with the openness of the Buddhists to invite and involve me in their celebration although they were aware that I was not a Buddhist and had no intention of becoming one. They were pleased with my willingness to participate in their worship, even though I do not function in their symbol system.

At the end of it all no one had lost his or her faith; Buddhism had not collapsed, nor the world around us. All that it led to was the forging of another link of friendship and understanding.

Can interfaith marriages be held in church? I have had requests from young people, and every time when I refused because of church regulations I had a sense of shame, because I felt that I had presented a Christianity to them that is nervous and insecure, afraid if someone who does not believe exactly as we do were to be part of our ceremony. I was ashamed that our Christian faith is presented as not strong enough to co-exist with another faith under the same roof and come to terms with it. Ashamed also because of the total lack in our approach of the giving and receiving of hospitality, which was so spontaneously evident in that Japanese Buddhist temple.

We need a theology that does not turn the Christian faith into a fortress. We need a theology that can interact with other ways of believing and being. More than anything else, we need a theology that makes us hospitable. An inhospitable theology cannot produce hospitable people.

Many questions remain. Children, religious education, practice of religion at home and so on demand urgent attention from religious communities. They are insoluble problems only if the communities see themselves as rival communities, rather than as the one human community with different stories to tell of their encounter with reality. They are not the same story, nor do they cancel one another out. Religious communities owe this to the coming generations. Otherwise a whole new group within the human community, the increasing number of interfaith couples and their children, will have to continue to fend for themselves.

If, however, religious traditions find ways to deal with the phenomenon creatively, they may well be exploring ways of handling their own future. For while the fortress mentality is still alive and well in all religions, the world, as Wilfred Cantwell Smith put it, "has gone irreversibly interfaith"!

NOTES

[1] *Pro Dialogo*, no. 96, 1997, 3.
[2] *Op. cit.*
[3] In the Old Testament, while honouring the parents is included in the ten commandments, detailed regulations had to be drawn in relation to marriage, divorce, remarriage, etc. In the New Testament, even in the words attributed to Jesus that marriage is indissoluble, an exemption clause is included on the ground of adultery. Paul, in his letter to the church in Corinth, gives advice, also on interfaith marriages, that takes actual situations into consideration. It can be shown by examining the teachings on marriage in other religions too that the laws concerning marriage relationships, in view of the reality of human nature, are not dogmatic but pragmatic. They are designed primarily for the well-being of the persons in marriage and the family.

7. Dialogue or Mission: Can the Tension Be Resolved?

During the twelve years I served the WCC in the dialogue programme I had the opportunity to conduct seminars and workshops, and to give lectures on the subject of dialogue in several countries. I have also spoken during these years to a great many students at the Ecumenical Institute at Bossey and to visitors to the Ecumenical Centre. Looking back on this experience, I believe that the most troubling question in relation to dialogue for the church is the issue of "mission". This is of course no great discovery, and will hardly surprise anyone who has even a cursory familiarity with the faith and history of the church.

Christianity is what we call a "missionary religion". That simply means that it is one of those religions which have a "message" to share with the rest of humanity. Islam, for example, is also such a religion, with an inbuilt conviction that its message is for the whole of humankind. Deeper reflection will show that in fact all religions, with the exception of what are known as "traditional religions", where religion is deeply embedded as part of a particular community's specific understanding and way of life, are "missionary" in character. Therefore, being a missionary religion is not, as some seem to think, a special "problem" of those religions that arose in the Semitic culture. Buddhism, born from Hinduism, within the heart of Asian culture, is one of the most successful missionary religions of the world. From its tentative beginnings in North India, it has now become the major religion of Sri Lanka, Myanmar (Burma), Thailand, Indochina and all of East Asia, including China, Japan and Korea. The Lord Buddha undertook preaching missions and called upon his disciples to share the message. So did the founders of Sikhism, Jainism and other Indian religions.

Hinduism, however, functions both as a traditional religion and as a missionary one. There is a side to Hinduism that simply has to do with all the religious experiences of the land of the Indus river. Although Hinduism, because of this self-understanding, has for the most part been a tolerant religion, at certain periods of history there have also been rival missions within India among Hindus, Jains and Buddhists, with conversions and re-conversions, which even included episodes of religious persecution. Today, while some Hindus, including members of the Hindu nationalist political party, still maintain that their religion constitutes all religious expressions in the land mass called India, some other branches of Hinduism undertake wide-ranging missionary activities in all parts of the world.

We need to remind ourselves of this reality in order to put the issue of mission in the right perspective. Many tend to confuse the problem of the excesses and insensitivities that marked the expansion of Christianity during the colonial period with the deeper issues of Christian witness and mission. There is much that must be rejected and even condemned in the collusion between religion and political power, especially during the European colonization of the world in the 18th and 19th centuries. But there is also a different understanding of mission according to which Christians are not the missionary "villains" of the world nor Christianity the only religion with the inner compulsion to engage in missionary activity. Most religions have a missionary dimension, even though there are a variety of ways in which it is expressed.

Christianity has been unapologetically missionary in character from its very origins. The gospels say that Jesus began his ministry proclaiming the breaking in of the reign of God and calling on people to "repent and believe in the good news". Until he was arrested and condemned to death, Jesus had been going about carrying out his mission in the towns and villages, preaching, teaching and bringing wholeness into the lives of people. Following his death, when the disciples had the experience of the risen Christ, they too, in the power of the Holy Spirit, felt the urgency to "bear witness" to the risen Lord, often at the risk of imprisonment and even of losing their lives. Paul was convinced, through his encounter with the risen Christ, that the in-breaking of the new order of existence that has overcome all the old walls of division must be preached to the very ends of the earth!

Matthew sums up these convictions as the grand finale of his gospel story in words he ascribes to Jesus himself: "All authority in heaven and on earth has been given to me. Go therefore and make disciples of all nations, baptizing them in the name of the Father and of the Son and of the Holy Spirit, and teaching them to obey everything that I have commanded you. And remember, I am with you always, to the end of the age" (28:18-20 NRSV). Here Matthew brings together in a single passage all the elements of the understanding of what is involved in Christian mission: "all authority in heaven and on earth", "preaching and teaching", "making disciples", "baptizing them in the name of the Trinity" and the assurance of Christ's own constant presence in all missionary activity.

Dialogue challenged

It should have been no surprise, then, that when the dialogue programme, formally initiated within the WCC in 1971, was reported on at the Nairobi assembly in 1975, it met stiff resistance from those who feared that engagement in dialogue might lead to a betrayal of Christian mission. The strong opposition to dialogue at Nairobi stemmed from what I have elsewhere called "the three classical fears" of the missionary movement: "syncretism", "compromising the uniqueness of Christ" and "loss of the urgency of mission".

The issue became so divisive that the report on "seeking community", which argued for "dialogue" as a new way of relating to people of other faith traditions, had to be referred back to the drafting committee for revision, taking account of the "reservation" that had been expressed.

Nairobi was the first WCC assembly I attended, and I was there as an advisor to Faith and Order and to make a brief presentation at the unity plenary. I was not part of the section on seeking community, which dealt with dialogue issues. Quite unexpectedly I found myself deeply involved in the dialogue debate because I was able to "hear" in some of the interventions the open-air preacher at the Jaffna stadium, denying any relationship between God and our Hindu neighbours. The setting of the debate was global, but the theology and the objections to a new relationship were exactly the same.

The Nairobi controversy is now an old story; much has already been written on it. There is no need to retell it or to relive all the emotion-packed drama it entailed. But it is important to note that the "preamble", added to make the original report acceptable to those who were antagonistic towards it, brought back all the traditional undertones of and convictions on mission:

> • We are all agreed that the *skandalon* (stumbling block) of the gospel will always be with us... While we do seek wider community with people of other faiths, cultures and ideologies, we do not think that there will ever be a time in history when the tension will be resolved between belief in Jesus Christ and unbelief.
> • We should also make a proper distinction between the division created by the judging word of God and the division of sin.
> • We are all agreed that the great commission of Jesus Christ which asks us to go out into all the world and make disciples of all nations, and to baptize them in the triune name, should not be abandoned or betrayed, disobeyed or compromised, neither should it be misused.
> • We are all opposed to any all forms of syncretism, incipient, nascent or developed, if we mean by syncretism conscious or unconscious human attempts to create a new religion composed of elements taken from different religions.
> • We view the future of the church's mission as full of hope, for it is not upon human efforts that our hope is based, but upon the power and promise of God.[1]

In Asia, cows and goats are given what I had always thought of as "prescribed freedom". Often a loop at one end of a long rope is put around the neck of a cow; the other end is tied to a tree trunk. This gives the cow considerable "freedom" to move around. The rope, however, is not too long and the freedom is limited. The cow is effectively prevented from eating up the plants we want to protect and, of course, the neighbour's garden!

When I first came to Switzerland, I thought that the cows there had much greater freedom (though no cow can be more free than the ones on the main streets of Madras or Bombay!). It was much later that I realized that the innocent-looking, simple, low wire fences around the grazing area are fed with a low electric charge. Any cow that attempted to go beyond would receive a minor electric shock. They too learn not to stray beyond prescribed limits.

The "preamble" at Nairobi put a noose around the neck of the dialogue report, for fear that it might devour Matthew 28! For those who attempted to set limits to dialogue, the great commission was the cornerstone of the missionary enterprise of the church. Anything which even vaguely challenged it undermined the very rationale of the church.

This meant that on the plenary floor of the assembly we had no dialogue on dialogue. Fear and suspicion marked the debate. The Asians who were advocating the new relationship tried to explain that they were not against mission, only for a new context and relationship for Christian witness. Lynn de Silva from Sri Lanka, for example, argued that a new context for Christian witness was necessary "to repudiate the arrogance, aggression and negativism of our evangelistic crusades which have obscured the gospel and caricatured it as an aggressive and militant religion", making "proclamation ineffective and irrelevant" to the people of Asia.

Russell Chandran from India (who was my teacher and principal of the theological college where I first studied theology) tried to discern the role of the great commission in the debate, and made a direct appeal to that concern: "We would like our brethren [*sic*] who are concerned about the commitment to the great commission of our Lord and the dangers of syncretism to be willing to listen to the testimony and insights of those who have more knowledge of other faiths and *are in no way less committed to Jesus Christ and his mission*," he said. "We plead that they avoid the mistake of making judgments on the basis of traditional doctrines, without knowledge of other people and their faiths, *and thus failing to grow into the fullness of Christ*."[2]

It must be noted that both Lynn de Silva and Russell Chandran affirmed Christian witness; they were only asking for a new understanding of what it involved in the light of living with people of other faiths. But many from the mission-minded Western churches remained unconvinced. They felt that a fence, preferably with a low electric charge, was indeed called for!

Writing about it after the assembly, David E. Jenkins, bishop of Durham, said that the call to "dialogue" by the churches which lived in religiously plural societies led "to an outcry about syncretism and betrayal of the gospel". And of the preamble, he added: "The response of the drafting committee to this outcry left many Asians and others feeling that their insights and convictions were being trampled on or betrayed."[3]

I did not want to go into the Nairobi dialogue debate for fear of repeating what is already well known. But it was my first assembly and I was myself drawn into the debate, defending the dialogue concern. The impressions remain vivid. The differences that surfaced during the debate led to the decision that a consultation representing the different voices heard in Nairobi should be convened to try to resolve the mission-dialogue tension.

Attempts to resolve the tension

The story of the attempts to resolve the tension between mission and dialogue within the WCC is a fascinating one, but all I wish to document are the results of it.

The first attempt to deal with the issue was made in Chiang Mai, Thailand, in April 1977 at the meeting called to continue the Nairobi debate and to clarify the issues. I was invited to present a paper on the "Nature, Purpose and Goals of Interfaith Dialogue". It was only at Chiang Mai that I fully realized how, while the context of the large assembly and the presence of the mass media had highlighted the controversy and given it much publicity, the fundamental issue that gave rise to the Nairobi debate had been with the church from the beginning. I also realized that it was the same issue that I had been grappling with as a young adult in relation to our next-door neighbours: What do we do theologically with the reality that my neighbour is a believing and praying person with a spiritual history, and often giving an undeniable witness to a life lived in God?

Much was done at Chiang Mai to clarify the concepts of "mission", "dialogue", "syncretism" and so on, and to come up with the celebrated *Guidelines on Dialogue*, which became the basis for sets of guidelines drawn up by local churches. But for me the most important contribution of the Chiang Mai meeting lies elsewhere. It pointed out to the churches that in the "dialogue-mission problematic" the church is faced not so much with choices and preferences, but with some fundamental issues of theology and self-understanding.

The *Guidelines* made clear that when Christians are engaged in dialogue they cannot avoid "asking themselves penetrating questions about the place of these people in the activity of God in history". Such questions, it continued, were not theoretical; they arose from the desire to know "what God may be doing in the lives of hundreds of millions of men and women who live in and seek community together with Christians, but along different ways".

It also raised some questions on which agreement was "more difficult and sometimes impossible", and commended them for "further fruitful discussions". Questions such as:

> What is the relation between the universal creative/redemptive activity of God towards all humankind and the particular creative/redemptive activity of God in the history of Israel and in the person and work of Jesus Christ?
>
> Are Christians to speak of God's work in the lives of all men and women only in tentative terms of hope that they may experience something of him, or more positively in terms of God's self-disclosure to people of living faiths and ideologies and in the struggle of human life?
>
> How are Christians to find from the Bible criteria in their approach to people of other faiths and ideologies, recognizing, as they must, the authority accorded to the Bible by Christians

of all centuries... [and knowing that] the partners in dialogue have other starting points and resources, both in holy books and traditions of teachings?

What is the biblical view and Christian experience of the operation of the Holy Spirit, and is it right and helpful to understand the work of God outside the church in terms of the doctrine of the Holy Spirit?[4]

I have developed one strand of the Nairobi debate through the Chiang Mai meeting to show that the real issue in the "dialogue or mission" controversy is not about relationships. Even the most mission-minded person today will agree that we should have an open, friendly and courteous relationship with our neighbours and that there is no place in mission for condemning the beliefs of others. In fact, a number of writers who may call themselves "conservative evangelicals" have written of the importance of dialogue, both as a way of relating to others and as an effective opening for the evangelistic mission. Bishop Lesslie Newbigin, who was insistent to the end on the importance of preaching the gospel message to others so that they "respond to Christ, in whom alone God's final saving act was revealed in history", argued that both dialogue and evangelism have their rightful places within the life of the church.

Thus the tension was not about whether we should engage in dialogue or in mission. Rather, it was about God and our neighbour. Are we in mission because God has not revealed God's self to the neighbour or in spite and indeed because of it?

The evidence that this in fact was the issue is to be seen in the second attempt to resolve the tension at the WCC's next assembly, in Vancouver (1983). The controversy here was no less acute, and followed much the same pattern as at Nairobi: the presentation of the report, its rejection, a re-draft to accommodate the objections, and disappointment on the part of those who wanted to see a theological breakthrough.

The sentence that created the controversy at Vancouver read: "While affirming the uniqueness of the birth, life, death and resurrection of Jesus to which we bear witness, we recognize God's creative work in the religious experience of people of other faiths." The first part of the sentence with the emphasis on "uniqueness" and the intention to "bear witness" was obviously meant to allay fears about what followed. But in spite of it, recognizing God's creative work "in the religious experience of the people of other faiths" became deeply controversial. Because of concerted opposition the report had to be sent back to the committee, as happened in Nairobi. In addition to the many suggestions made on the floor of the assembly, the drafting committee directly received no fewer than 68 written proposals for the revision of this one sentence, and thus set what must have been an ecumenical record for the number of suggestions made for the revision of part of a sentence at an assembly!

The redrafted version read: "... we recognize God's creative work in the seeking for religious truth among people of other faiths". Thus while the revised text was willing to allow for God's creative action in the *seeking* within other faiths, it discounted such activity on the part of God in their *finding*. That can happen only through Christ, presented to others through Christian mission.[5]

Listening to the Vancouver debate it appeared to me that some felt it necessary to put a noose even around God's neck and tie the other end to the tree trunk of Christian mission, or at least put up a low-charge electric fence to prevent too much roaming around on the part of God!

So the "tension" remained, even though 12 years earlier Dialogue had been officially initiated as a programme, and it had by now become an acceptable activity in the WCC and many of its member churches.

A step forward

The next attempt to resolve that tension had to be taken into the very bastion of the mission-oriented constituencies of the ecumenical movement, the world mission conference (also referred to as the conference on world mission and evangelism). First called in 1910 in Edinburgh, Scotland, the conference, which met approximately every seven to ten years, attempted to bring together all the major voices on mission at the time it met, and all major mission agencies around the globe.

The tenth world mission conference met in San Antonio, Texas, in May-June 1989. For the first time in history, following the practice at WCC assemblies since Nairobi, guests of other faiths had been invited to a world mission conference. There was a measure of expectation that the mission conference would speak with some clarity on the subject that had plagued two assemblies. "Christian relationship to people of other faiths" had already been identified as one of the four major issues of the conference.

There were also warning signals. The April 1989 issue of the influential periodical on mission, *International Bulletin on Missionary Research*, devoted its pages to issues likely to occupy the world mission conference. Its editorial and two main articles concentrated on the challenge of dialogue-related theology to the understanding and practice of mission. In the lead article, Lesslie Newbigin warned the conference of the "contemporary output of the interfaith industry". He concluded the article by reminding the participants of the theology of religions debate at the last two WCC assemblies: "The WCC has been asked, at two general assemblies, to accept statements that seem to call in question the uniqueness, decisiveness and centrality of Jesus Christ. It has resisted. If in the pull of the strong current, it should agree to go with the present tide, it would become an irrelevance in the spiritual struggles that lie ahead of us. I pray and believe that it will not" (p.54).

At that time I was in charge of the dialogue programme of the WCC and helping with the theological explorations on "My Neighbour's Faith and Mine – Theological Discoveries through Interfaith Dialogue".

I had known Bishop Newbigin from the time I was a student. We were good friends. As those who had known and worked with the late bishop would testify, he was a man of great intellectual ability and clarity of thought, an outstanding preacher, a lucid writer and an outstanding leader of the ecumenical movement. He had contributed significantly to the integration of the International Missionary Council in the WCC at the New Delhi assembly. As the first director of the WCC's Commission on World Mission and Evangelism (CWME) he had served the ecumenical movement well. He had also served as the bishop of the Madurai-Ramnad and Madras dioceses of the Church of South India and had had direct contacts with people of other faith traditions.

Newbigin also represented, however, a stream of mission theology that was at odds with the theological rethinking that was going on within the dialogue stream. The bishop and I had crossed swords several times on the "dialogue issue", including an animated face-to-face debate on dialogue and mission at a Graduate School session of the Ecumenical Institute in Bossey. But our disagreements were always in a spirit of dialogue.

The Bulletin, with the bishop's interpretation of the assembly debates, had been made widely available to conference participants. Even though he had not been one of the conference speakers, he was requested to give an address outside the official programme. The bishop and I were brought together to present our views at a press conference on what were euphemistically called the "critical issues" facing the conference.

The underlying theological issue, however, was not one that could be argued out at a press conference, with all its possibilities for misunderstanding and even misrepresentation. I decided to keep a low profile. Asian wisdom demands that one should not only choose one's battles but also the battle-fields. The real struggle had to take place in the section meeting of the conference that dealt with dialogue issues, and the committee that drafted the report. The bishop, unfortunately, was not able to engage more directly in these discussions. He had been flown in for a few days to help prevent possible compromises on one of the streams of the theology of mission, which called for the "direct evangelization and conversion of those who do not believe in Christ" – as it was put by one of the participants in the debate.

The San Antonio report on witness among people of other faiths, however, showed that despite Newbigin's warnings the dialogue "current" had in fact pushed the churches to a more open approach to the religious life of our neighbours. It clearly stated that "our mission to witness to Jesus Christ can never be given up". But having affirmed the rightful place of Christian witness, it did make several statements that went well beyond what previous mission conferences and assemblies had been able to say. For example, it said:

> In reaffirming the "evangelistic mandate" of the ecumenical movement, we would like to emphasize that we may never claim to have a full understanding of God's truth: we are only the recipients of God's grace. Our ministry of witness among people of other faiths presupposes our presence with them, sensitivity to their deepest faith commitments and experience, willingness to be their servants for Christ's sake, affirmation of what God has done and is doing among them, and love for them. Since God's mystery in Christ surpasses our understanding and since our knowledge of God's saving power is imperfect, we Christians are called to be witnesses to others, not judges of them. We also affirm that it is possible to be non-aggressive and missionary at the same time – that it is, in fact, the only way of being truly missionary...

Having thus set the stage for more open relationships, the San Antonio report also opened some new windows for the Protestant mission theology that had dominated the ecumenical missionary movement:

> ...We cannot point to any other way of salvation than Jesus Christ; at the same time we cannot set limits to the saving power of God...
>
> ...In dialogue we are invited to listen, in openness to the possibility that the God we know in Jesus Christ may encounter us also in the lives of our neighbours of other faiths.

San Antonio also confirmed the growing consensus developing within the churches on mission and dialogue: "Dialogue has its own place and integrity and is neither opposed to nor incompatible with witness or proclamation."

It further said, "We recognize that both witness and dialogue presuppose two-way relationships. We affirm that witness does not preclude dialogue but invites it, and that dialogue does not preclude witness but extends and deepens it..." And, as has already been mentioned, San Antonio also sought to refrain from advocating a theology that would set limits to God's saving presence outside.

But did it succeed in resolving the theological "tension" involved in the positions it took? Let the report speak for itself:

> ...we are well aware that these convictions and the ministry of witness (to Jesus Christ) stand in tension with what we have affirmed about God being present in and at work in people of other faiths; *we appreciate this tension, and do not attempt to resolve it.*[6]

San Antonio went as far as it could go. It did not want to set limits to God's saving presence elsewhere, but at the same time it was unequivocal in its claim that Jesus Christ is the saviour of all humankind. It was honest in admitting that it did not seek to resolve the tension involved. It could not have in any case because there was no agreed theological basis to do so.

In November 1996 when the next (eleventh) world mission conference met in Salvador, Bahia, Brazil, it sought to make a contribution to yet another of the difficult issues that have preoccupied the ecumenical movement since its inception: "Gospel and Cultures". From the very beginning, there was a recognition of the close link between religion and culture. Asian and African cultures, for example, are intricately interwoven with the religious reality. No attempt to deal theologically with cultures can avoid grappling with Christian theological assumptions in regard to other religious traditions. Therefore, it was reasonable to expect that it might go further in dealing with the issue that San Antonio had consciously decided to leave unresolved.

But Salvador contributed nothing to advance the discussion. It affirmed and encouraged dialogue, and gave descriptive accounts, with concrete examples, of the factors that prevent dialogue in local congregations and of possibilities that were already present. It also suggested practical steps to encourage dialogue at the local level. But on the unresolved theological issue it had nothing new to say.

Again, at first it recognizes the issue and appears to be prepared to deal with it:

> The increasingly multi-religious nature of many societies raises major theological questions which are reflected also in the reactions of people in local congregations. The presence of God in societies, cultures and religions independent of the presence of a church is one such issue. Aboriginal people in Australia, for example, witness powerfully to such experience. Early Christian theologians like Justin Martyr spoke of "the seeds of the word" among the cultures of the world. Many today recognize that Christ transcends time and space and reveals himself to those whom he chooses... This makes it possible for Christians to become open to the truth revealed in other cultures and traditions...

And then, a cautious return to San Antonio:

> ...But in so doing, a Christian community should never lose the centre of its faith: Jesus Christ, crucified and risen... It is important to reaffirm the statement of the San Antonio world mission conference "that we cannot point to any other way of salvation than Jesus Christ; at the same time we cannot set limits to the saving power of God". With San Antonio, we affirm that "these convictions and the ministry of witness stand in tension with what we have affirmed about God being present in and at work in people of other faiths; we appreciate this tension, and do not attempt to resolve it".[7]

The coordinator of the conference, Christopher Duraisingh, who also wrote the evaluative account of the conference under the attractive title "Salvador: A Signpost of the New in Mission", had to admit that "while more than one section touched upon this issue [of dialogue and mission] Salvador did not go beyond what San Antonio said".[8] Thus, as far as the mission-dialogue issue was concerned, there was no sign-post of "the new" in mission!

The story of the attempts to resolve the tension, especially within the ministry of the WCC, would remain incomplete without reference to the work done within the dialogue programme itself. This took the form of a four-year study process on "My Neighbour's Faith and Mine – Theological Discoveries through Interfaith Dialogue", which culminated in two meetings on the theology of religions, both held at Baar, near Zurich, Switzerland. Even though these meetings had representatives from the Roman Catholic, Orthodox and Protestant branches of the church and from different regions of the world, they do not have the same "authority" as the assemblies and world conferences, which are more truly representative of the spectrum of opinion of the church on any issue.

The Baar declarations, however, indicate some of the directions in which one needed to move in seeking to deal with the theological issues related to mission and dialogue.

A theological understanding of religious plurality

A study of the "history of missions" and the mainstream "theologies of mission" will show that the church has never paid too much attention to the task of dealing theologically with religious plurality. This does not mean that there was no discussion of the issue. Indeed there were some deeply contentious discussions, as at the world mission conferences in Jerusalem (1928) and in Tambaram (Madras, 1938). There has also been a variety of approaches to other religions, ranging from rejecting them outright as "pagan" and as the very evidence of human rebellion against God, to seeing them as "partial", "incomplete" and "preparatory", awaiting their true fulfilment in the message of the gospel. The documents of the Second Vatican Council went much further in recognizing them as possible vehicles of God's salvific action, but of course, ultimately through the paschal mystery of Christ.[9]

These discussions, however, happen at the margins of the churches' mainline theology and doctrinal positions and have had no discernable effect on them. The doctrine of creation, for example, is rarely spelled out in the churches' theologies in terms of plurality, certainly not of religious plurality. In much of Protestant theology creation just sets the stage or becomes no more than a prelude to the "fall" and the consequent unfolding of the drama of salvation. An undeveloped theology of creation lies at the heart of the Protestant inability to deal with plurality. Today there is a new interest in creation, but it is more in relation to the natural environment than about the peoples who fill the earth.

At Baar theologians decided to deal with this issue. "Our theological understanding of religious plurality", says the Baar declaration, "begins with our faith in the one God who created all things, the living God, present and active in all creation from the beginning. The Bible testifies to God as God of all nations and peoples, whose love and compassion includes all humankind. We see in the covenant with Noah a covenant with all creation. We see his wisdom and justice extending to the ends of the earth as he guides the nations through their traditions of wisdom and understanding. God's glory penetrates the whole of creation."[10]

Such an affirmation of God as the creator of all that exists is of course part of classical theological affirmations. The psalmist's claim – "The earth is the Lord's and all that is in it, the world, and those who live in it" (24:1) – is part of the liturgy of all the churches. What Baar did was to draw the theological consequences of making such an affirmation for the earth's peoples:

> People have at all times and in all places responded to the presence and activity of God among them, and have given their witness to their encounters with the living God. In this testimony they speak both of seeking and of having found salvation, or wholeness, or enlightenment, or divine guidance, or rest, or liberation.
>
> We therefore take this witness with the utmost seriousness and acknowledge that among all the nations and peoples there has always been the saving presence of God.

In this affirmation Baar was responding to the Vancouver statement allowing for the "seeking" but not the "finding" of God on the part of peoples of other faiths. This issue was discussed at some length at Baar, and participants felt that to insist that the knowledge of God is available to people only when they have accepted Christ is not only a statement about other religions but also about God. It was inconceivable that the God of love, compassion and grace, whom we have come to know in Jesus Christ, would not have a relationship with people who are God's own creation. Moreover, in contemporary thinking the anthropomorphic ideas of God are giving way to an understanding of God as Being itself in whom all life is rooted, nurtured and being drawn towards its intended purpose.

The Baar declaration, therefore, went further than any of the previous WCC statements to affirm the plurality of religious traditions as being within God's providence and the locus of God's presence and activity:

> We see the plurality of religious traditions as both the result of the manifold ways in which God has related to peoples and nations as well as a manifestation of the richness and diversity of humankind... Where there is truth and wisdom in their teachings, and love and holiness in their living, this, like any wisdom, insight, knowledge, understanding, love and holiness that is found among us, is the gift of the Holy Spirit. We also affirm that God is with them as they struggle, along with us, for justice and liberation.
>
> This conviction that God as creator of all is present and active in the plurality of religions makes it inconceivable to us that God's saving activity could be confined to any one continent, cultural type, or group of peoples. A refusal to take seriously the many and diverse religious testimonies to be found among the nations and peoples of the whole world amounts to disowning the biblical testimony to God as creator of all things and father of humankind...
>
> It is our Christian faith in God which challenges us to take seriously the whole realm of religious plurality. We see this not so much as an obstacle to be overcome, but rather as an opportunity for deepening our encounter with God and with our neighbours as we await the fulfilment when "God will be all in all".

I have quoted substantial parts of the Baar declaration because, within the ecumenical family, it represents an attempt to make a significant breakthrough on the question of religious plurality. We had brought together for this meeting a representative group of theologians of the churches, so that the statement, though not "official", would be based on the reflections of persons who are themselves committed to the church. They also had an informed understanding of the churches' own positions and hesitations on the questions involved.

Several days of struggle with the issue left the group with the conviction that we can no longer hold a theology that maintains God's absence in the religious life of our neighbours without doing serious violence to the Christian understanding and experience of God.

Was Baar overly "romantic" about religious traditions and did it ignore the ways in which religion itself can become a manifestation of the rebellion against God?

Here some distinctions are called for. Karl Barth, in his early writings, took a negative view of all religions (including Christianity as a religion) because, in his view, God the "wholly Other", can only be known through God's self-revelation in history. Sinful humans cannot grasp God by their own efforts, and therefore any attempt to grasp God or claims to have had knowledge of God can only be part of human presumption and sin. Religions are, therefore, a part of the rebellion of human beings against the transcendental Other.

Religions were also seen by Hendrik Kraemer, who interpreted Barth for missions, as "totalitarian systems" or "totalitarian apprehensions of reality", by Hendrik which he meant that all religions hold out views of life and reality that are inherent, inter-related "wholes". In his view we cannot look at some aspects of a religion and say, "Here, in this dimension, we see the action of the Holy Spirit."

The logical conclusion of this was that all religions, which are other than a response of faith to God's gracious self-revelation, both in their "heights" and "depths", represent no more than mere *human* "aspirations" and "sin". Based on this conviction Kraemer, in Tambaram, strongly resisted all attempts to see the gospel as the "fulfilment" of other religions or even of their hopes and aspirations. The gospel, in this view, is in total "discontinuity" with religions. The in-breaking of God's reign into human life constitutes a "crisis" for every human life. As a crisis, it does not fulfil but demands the response of "repentance" and "faith". Thus the gospel, far from being the fulfilment of any religion, is a challenge to, and a judgment on, all religion.

Barth, in his essay "The Light and the Lights", and Kraemer in his later writings modified this totally dismissive view of religions, but by then the foundations for an assessment of and a relationship to religions had already been laid within the Protestant missionary movement.

I have recalled this theological background, familiar to many, only to show that it was not just Matthew 28 and the fear of syncretism that lay behind the dialogue-mission controversy at Nairobi and Vancouver. Those who knew something of mission history and the earlier controversies would have seen the spirits of Barth and Kraemer hovering over the plenary hall!

The real problem then is twofold. The first has to do with the urgency of mission as enjoined by the great commission. The second, less openly articulated today because we have become more friendly with people of other faiths (who were also physically present as "guests" at both assemblies), is the belief that all religions which are not a response to God's self-revelation in Christ are, in the last analysis, sinful; they represent, not the spiritual heights which human beings can attain, but the sinful rebellion against God that began in Genesis 3.

Baar begged to differ.

Baar was prepared to live with a more complex understanding of religion and of the possibility within it of rebelling against as well as responding to God's love. Thus while affirming the presence of the Holy Spirit where there is "wisdom, insight, knowledge, understanding, love and holiness", it went on to say: "Any affirmation of the positive qualities of wisdom, love, compassion and spiritual insights in the world's religious traditions must also speak with honesty and with sadness of the human wickedness and folly that is also present in all religious communities. We must recognize the ways in which religion has functioned too often to support systems of oppression and exclusion."

The difference that Baar made to the discussion is that, faced with the ambiguity of all religions, it refused to run away, but rather called for discernment in the Spirit to seek to understand the purposes of God within this ambiguity. "Any adequate theology of religions," it maintained, "must deal with human wickedness and sin, with disobedience to spiritual insight and failure to live in accordance with the highest ideals. Therefore we are continuously challenged by the Spirit to discern the wisdom and purposes of God [within this ambiguity]."

Baar, thus, sought to provide a bold answer to what had to be left as a question in the *Guidelines on Dialogue*:

> We are clear, therefore, that a positive answer must be given to the question raised in the *Guidelines on Dialogue* (1979) "Is it right and helpful to understand the work of God outside the church in terms of the Holy Spirit" (para. 23). We affirm unequivocally that God the Holy Spirit has been at work in the life and traditions of peoples of living faiths.
>
> Further we affirm that it is within the realm of the Spirit that we may be able to interpret the truth and goodness of other religions and distinguish the "things that differ", so that our "love may abound more and more, with knowledge and all discernment" (Phil. 1:9-10).

These were directions in mission theology that would have helped to resolve the "tension", but the assemblies and mission conferences would not touch them; they opened up a theological minefield.

Christology and religious plurality

Also, at Baar, Christology proved the most difficult issue to tackle. The different confessional positions, especially in relation to Christ's saving work among the nations, had their own particularity and emphases, demanding a deeper dialogue among Christians before the issue of Christ and other faiths might be looked at.

The Roman Catholics went some way in resolving the tension by insisting, on the one hand, that the "Christ event is for us the clearest expression of the salvific will of God in all human history." On the other, as the Vatican II documents and their contemporary interpreters have done, they did not insist that repentance and belief in Christ in one's life-time were essential for anyone to be saved. It is the belief that such change of allegiance to Christ is necessary for salvation that puts an enormous burden on some sections of the church to "reach the unreached" before they "perish". The following part of the Baar statement reflects the Roman Catholic point of entry.

"This saving mystery [of Christ]," they held, "is mediated and expressed in many and various ways as God's plan unfolds towards its fulfilment. It may be available to those outside the fold of Christ (John 10:16) in ways we cannot understand, as they live faithful and truthful lives in their concrete circumstances and in the framework of the religious traditions which guide and inspire them."

Protestants too emphasized the universal character of God's saving act, and saw the Christ event as its focal point. "We affirm that in Jesus Christ, the incarnate word, the entire human family has been united to God in an irrevocable bond and covenant. The saving presence of God's activity in all creation and human history comes to its focal point in the event of Christ."

But if Baar wanted to make a contribution towards resolving the tension between dialogue and mission, it had to reflect, at even greater depth, on the relationship between God's saving presence in all of life, and what Christians believe God has done in Jesus Christ. Both San Antonio and Salvador refused to be drawn into making a theological statement on the relationship between the two. And the *Guidelines on Dialogue* could do no more than pose it as a question that must be faced. Yet, what one thinks about this makes all the difference to one's attitude to the religious life of one's neighbours. Therefore, while clearly confessing their faith in Jesus Christ, which shaped and ruled their own life, the Baar participants took a theological stand on the issue:

Because we have seen and experienced goodness, truth and holiness among followers of other paths and ways than that of Jesus Christ, we are forced to confront with total seriousness the question raised in the *Guidelines on Dialogue* (1979) concerning the universal creative and redemptive activity of God towards all humankind and the particular redemptive activity of God in the history of Israel and in the person and work of Jesus Christ (para. 23). We find ourselves recognizing a need to move beyond a theology which confines salvation to the explicit personal commitment to Jesus Christ.

Baar was not a representative gathering of churches, only a meeting of theologians who set themselves the task of exploring whether the theological issues that lie behind the unresolved tension between dialogue and mission could indeed be addressed for our day. And it did go some way towards that goal.

The world mission conference in Salvador met six years after Baar. But it failed to follow up and to build on what had been achieved.

Should the tension be resolved?

A basic issue here is whether we should at all try to resolve the tension. Isn't it wiser to leave some questions unanswered? Wasn't San Antonio right in saying, "We appreciate this tension, and do not attempt to resolve it"? Especially when we are dealing with the question of "salvation", where we confront an unfathomable mystery, is it reasonable to seek to find all the answers?

These are legitimate questions. I for one believe that we may well not find answers to all questions and that it is good to leave some issues unresolved. Life is indeed full of mystery. One does not dissect a rose to explore its beauty.

Then why take so much trouble over the question of "salvation?"

Beyond neutrality

Several years ago, when Willem Visser 't Hooft, first general secretary of the WCC, was living in retirement in Chêne-

Bougeries, Geneva, some of us who lived in the area used to meet with him periodically – what came to be known as the "ecumenical memory group". Ans van der Bent, the late director of the WCC Library, coordinated these meetings with great passion.

Ans was known for his unfailing zest. Quite often he would storm into my office as if the world around us were collapsing, only to tell me, full of righteous indignation, that somewhere in some meeting a word had been introduced into a report "that took the discussion back to where it was twenty years ago"!

"Yes, yes, yes...," he would say, shaking his head and going red in the face, "we need to move forward; otherwise the movement will perish, Wesley, yes... yes, the movement will perish!"

Ans was convinced that the challenges facing the ecumenical movement, especially in the interfaith area, were so enormous that we needed to press forward, building on what had already been done. "We are stagnating!", he would complain, looking at me as if I were the sole cause for such stagnation in the ecumenical movement! Then he would slam his hand on the chair and say, "We cannot afford it, yes... yes (he meant no, no) we cannot afford it."

Ans had matchless commitment to and unwavering faith in the ecumenical movement. He just could not suffer going back. Statements that took us backward greatly upset him.

I used to wonder if his car had a reverse gear.

The meetings he organized at the Visser 't Hooft residence were invaluable; we were able to hear first-hand accounts of the origins of the World Council of Churches and of the history of discussions on crucial ecumenical issues.

On one such occasion the question of dialogue came up, and in no time we were discussing the theology of religions. On this, Visser 't Hooft, like Lesslie Newbigin, shared the position held in the mainline missionary movement. When pressed to respond to the Hindu witness to the experience of grace within their tradition, he answered: "I do not know whether there is salvation in Hinduism. All I know is that in

Christ God wills to save all of humankind, and to this I am a witness."

The answer was adequate in some ways, but I had major problems with it. I remembered Kenneth Cragg's statement that Muslims have a "grievance" against us Christians, because while they have an opinion on who Jesus is (even if we may disagree with it), we Christians have no opinion on the Prophet. In all pluralistic situations Christians are constantly encountering religious life that witnesses to a two-way traffic between the divine and the human, at times expressing itself in selfless love and genuine holiness. Should we continue to say: "We don't know"?

As religious communities draw closer together and enter into deeper dialogue, Christians can no longer withhold opinion or refuse to enter into a meaningful relationship based on a more genuine appreciation of the religious life of our neighbours. That belonged to periods when religions were isolated from one another or even opposed to one another.

"Dr Visser 't Hooft," I said, after a few moments of respectful hesitation, "your generation had to move from theological hostility to theological neutrality about the faith of our neighbours. Our generation needs to move beyond neutrality."

Visser 't Hooft shook his head in directions that meant that he was not convinced. And then gave me a look that seemed to say: "Young man, I hope you know what you are talking about!"

Of course, in one sense, I cannot say whether there is "salvation" in Hinduism or not. My experience of God is rooted in Christ. But at the same time, I can no longer ignore the witness of my Hindu or Muslim neighbour to a life in God that has become profoundly meaningful to them. Since I believe in one God who is the source and sustenance of all of life, the Hindu and Muslim witness has to become a part of my theological data. Without it I cannot think theologically in a pluralistic world.

Now I understood my inner conflict as a young adult about our Hindu neighbours in KKS. It mattered to me then, long before I had come across the phrase "theology of religions", whether they were, in one way or another, in communion with God. Otherwise, I could not make sense of their life. I would not know how to relate to them as religious persons. I also needed to know whether the open-air preacher at the Jaffna stadium was right that they would indeed perish if they did not accept Christ and become Christians like us. It bothered me, since I could not see any prospect of their becoming part of the church, that there was no place in "heaven" for our Hindu neighbours.

But it is not just my personal struggle which, over the years, I have overcome by unlearning many things I had learned at the Sunday school. It is, more importantly, a theological dilemma that faces Christians in all pluralistic situations. As long as the churches maintain a studied silence on this question, our relationships and the quality of dialogue with neighbours of other faiths will remain tentative, half-hearted and devoid of depth or meaning.

The challenge we face

For all its efforts, Baar did nothing more than scratch the surface of the problem. The questions related to mission in pluralistic situations are much deeper and await much more honest and open discussions.

Why do I say this? My exposure to discussions of the issue at the assemblies and the mission conferences has convinced me that in church-related meetings mission discussions are as much "political" as theological – if they are ever theological. There are, it seems to me, too many "no-go areas" in church discussions on missions. The "uniqueness of Christ", "syncretism", "negative evaluation of other religions" and the "missionary mandate" constitute the four sides of the fence, with red flags on them. One cannot breach any one of these without receiving the "shock" of an outcry of "betrayal".

Therefore when mission-dialogue discussions deal with theological issues, one can almost predict who will speak and what position they will take. There is a troubling silence on the part of many others who should be involved. The net effect of this is that missiology is perhaps the one area of theology where there are too many loose ends with no one wanting to pick them up for fuller exploration.

Why are we in mission? Is it because God is present with our neighbour or because God is absent?

If God is absent in the life of our neighbour, what do we make of our belief that God loves all people and that they live and move and have their being in God? If God is present, what is the relationship of our message to the religious life of our neighbours?

What are we after in mission? When is mission completed?

What is mission about? Is it about discipleship, healing, new life or "salvation"?

If it is about salvation, what constitutes salvation, and what are the signs of being saved?

These are profound issues. I do not say that they have not been tackled, or that these questions should be satisfactorily dealt with or answered before we can talk about or engage in mission. But what *is* troubling is that mission discussions, on too many occasions, seem to pretend that these questions do not exist or need not be taken seriously. No wonder discussions on mission, especially in church situations, are often rhetorical, and do not address the real issues that plague the understanding and practice of mission in our day.

The question "What constitutes salvation?" reminds me of a conversation I had many years ago with a Hindu fellow-traveller during a train journey. Our conversation focused on *Saiva Siddhanta*, a system of metaphysics which informs and undergirds Hinduism in Sri Lanka. Let me conclude with an account of our meeting; I believe it has something to tell us about mission, dialogue – and the need to go beyond neutrality.

Now that you are saved...

When I was a young minister in Jaffna in northern Sri Lanka, quite often I had to go to Colombo, the capital of the country, where we had the Methodist headquarters. The journey in those days took nearly eight hours. Jaffna had a predominantly Hindu population; I often found myself sitting next to a Hindu, and engaging in conversation on a variety of issues.

On one such journey I was seated next to an elderly Hindu person who obviously had an in-depth knowledge and experience of his faith. We were having an interesting conversation on *Saiva Siddhanta* when we had to listen to a testimony.

Several young persons were walking up and down the train, engaged in "train evangelism". They would get into a train with a return ticket to the next stop. During the onward journey they would go down the train distributing evangelistic pamphlets, and giving "a personal witness" where appropriate. They would get off the train at the next stop and wait for the train back to repeat the performance on the return journey.

Soon the Hindu friend and I had the immediate company of one of the young persons. I was in shirt sleeves and was not recognizable as a Methodist minister. After giving us a tract, the young man offered to give us his testimony.

He had been drinking, smoking; he was often disobedient to his parents. He had led a bad life. Then he was introduced to Christ, and his life was transformed. He knew he was saved, and he was making the offer of salvation in Christ to us also.

There was no doubt that the young man had in fact undergone an experience of transformation. His testimony was genuine and sincere.

Once the young man had left us, I wondered what all this had meant to my Hindu fellow-traveller. "How did that come across to you?", I asked him.

He was looking out of the train window, pondering, watching the trees appear for a moment to disappear from our view in no time. Then we had more trees, buildings, vacant land, groups of people, cattle, children chasing one another! Everything was fleeting; nothing stayed for more than a moment as the train sped towards Jaffna and then on to KKS, its final destination.

Did the testimony of the young man force my Hindu friend into a reflection on the fleeting nature of human life?

No, it turned out that he was in fact thinking about the young man and his testimony. "How old do you think this young man would be?", he asked me.

"Well, perhaps sixteen or seventeen," I answered.

There was silence. And then, the question: "Now that he has found salvation at the age of seventeen, what is he going to do with the rest of his life?" I was dumbfounded.

I often recall this when people talk about salvation. What is it that we are offering to the Hindu through our witness? How is it heard and understood within a world-view that has so little in common with ours? How can our witness be incorporated into a spiritual tradition that has stood the test of time through many centuries?

While it must be true that the young man had in fact "found Christ" and that had helped him to "repent" of his "sins" and to live a "new life" (the key words of the testimony), what was the nature of "salvation" he was offering to the sixty-some year old person who had been steeped in his scriptures, seen the ups and downs of life, had a Saiva Siddhantic view of reality and would perhaps testify to many moments of awareness of standing in the presence of God?

Where was the "connection"?

The Hindu was not frivolous when he asked, "What is he going to do with the rest of his life?" For him salvation was a life-time pursuit. In Saiva Siddhanta, the school of Hinduism to which he belonged, there is a strong sense of the soul's alienation from God because of the sin of self-centredness *(anavam)*. God, however, out of God's love and grace *(arul)* accompanies the soul through its life and its life-experiences and, if necessary, through many lives, in order to show the soul, through its very life-experiences, the futility of alienation from the very ground of its being. There will come a point when the soul realizes the utter futility of a life centred in itself rather than in God. This, in Siddhanta, is the true moment of "repentance" or "self-denial" when the soul, turning to God, is overwhelmed by a grace that had always been turned towards it and had been accompanying it through all its life-experiences to lure it unto Itself.

The songs or the psalms of the Saiva saints, especially the *tevarams* and the *tiruvasagam*, are full of the sense of awe, delight and rapture over the unrelenting love and grace of God that would not "let go" but patiently accompany the soul until it realizes where it actually belongs. They tell how the psalmist was lured into estrangement by a self-centred pursuit of life, and how God used that very life, and the experiences within it, to lure the psalmist back to God.

These psalms of the Saiva saints *(thevarams)* were what our next-door Hindu neighbours at KKS used to sing at their evening prayers.

This, then, was the belief that informed my fellow-traveller; it was the background of his question. For him, all the life-experiences that awaited the seventeen-year-old would teach him about life and its true goal, what is worth pursuing and what is not, what leads to "Life" and what does not. For the Hindu, the experience that the young man shared with us would be a part of the life-time process of turning and returning, of discovering how our very turning to God can be a self-centred move. Even a life-time may not be sufficient for us to discover the true nature of the hold "sin" *(anavam)* has on us and the abundance of the grace that pursues us all the time we are estranged from it!

To claim to have had salvation so expeditiously and so early is too much of a claim to make and too heavy a burden to carry for a seventeen-year-old, who has yet to meet the vicissitudes of life. The Hindu would agree that a person of seventeen should of course not drink, smoke or be disobedient to parents. If it took a dramatic religious experience for him to mend his ways, that is also understandable. But to talk of this in terms of "sin" and "salvation", even when it was a kind of turning one's life to God, is to trivialize both concepts and the glory that awaits a soul that finally finds itself in God.

This is not to undermine the experience of the young man. I myself had such an experience of Christ in my youth, though I was not saved from the same "sins". There indeed is an experience of Christ as one who challenges and transforms one's life.

And yet, the incident points to the complexity of what mission is all about. For all its good intentions and sincerity, mission that is not rooted in dialogue, and does not take the witness of our neighbours' life in God, can be misdirected, misunderstood and miss its purpose.

D.T. Niles once said at our clergy retreat that one of the crises facing mission is that we Christians are more convinced of "our need to be in mission" than of the "need of our neighbours to hear the gospel". Much mission takes place because of our need to be in mission; because the great commission has commanded us to go into all the world; because "woe to me if I do not preach the gospel". But if we truly believe that the gospel is for and about our neighbour, we may be more prepared to listen.

When my Hindu neighbour says that he or she has a life in God, it should become part of my theological agenda. It says something about God that has much to do with my mission. I can no longer stay neutral. I cannot say, "I don't know". Nor can I say that this constitutes "a tension I do not seek to resolve".

The "tension" itself constitutes the theological agenda for a new understanding of mission in pluralistic situations. It needs to be pursued within the practice and in the spirit of dialogue. Meaningful mission in the next millennium may well depend on the resolution of this tension. We have the resources; what we need more is courage.

NOTES

1 David M. Paton, ed., *Breaking Barriers, Nairobi 1975: The Official Report of the Fifth Assembly of the WCC*, London, SPCK, and Geneva, WCC, 1976, pp.73-76.
2 *Ibid.*, p.72 (italics added).

[3] David E. Jenkins, "Nairobi and the Truly Ecumenical: Contribution to a Discussion about the Subsequent Tasks of the WCC", *The Ecumenical Review*, vol. 28, July 1976, p.281.

[4] *Guidelines on Dialogue with People of Living Faiths and Ideologies*, WCC, Geneva, 1979, p.13.

[5] David Gill, ed. *Gathered for Life: Official Report, Sixth Assembly, World Council of Churches, Vancouver, Canada, 24 July-10 August 1983*, Grand Rapids, MI, Eerdmans, and Geneva, WCC, 1983, pp.31-42.

[6] Frederick R. Wilson, ed., *The San Antonio Report. Your Will Be Done: Mission in Christ's Way*, Geneva, WCC, 1990. See report of section I, esp. I:IV, pp.31-33 (italics added).

[7] Christopher Duraisingh, ed., *Called to One Hope: The Gospel in Diverse Cultures*, report of the 11th conference on world mission and evangelism, Salvador, Bahia, Brazil, Nov.-Dec. 1996, Geneva, WCC, 1998, pp.60-64.

[8] *Ibid.*, p.205.

[9] I have made a detailed historical-theological survey of the positions taken in the past and in contemporary literature in my book *Hindus and Christians: A Century of Protestant Ecumenical Thought*, Amsterdam, Rodopi, and Grand Rapids, MI, Eerdmans, 1991. It is a comprehensive study of the wider issue with Hinduism as the "test case".

[10] "Religious Plurality: Theological Perspectives and Affirmations", WCC Sub-unit on Dialogue with People of Living Faiths consultation, Baar, 1990. In Michael Kinnamon and Brian E. Cope, eds., *The Ecumenical Movement: An Anthology of Key Texts and Voices*, Geneva, WCC, and Grand Rapids, MI, Eerdmans, 1997, pp.417ff.